Case Studies

Stephen Rickerby

Published by Travel and Tourism Publishing Limited.

www.tandtpublishing.co.uk
info@tandtpublishing.co.uk

First published 2008

British Library Cataloguing in Publication Data is available from the British Library on request.

ISBN 978 0 9550190 6 7

Copyright notice

Designed and typeset by Sulwyn at Gomer Press
Cover image ©iStockphoto.com/Jim Jurica
Printed in the UK by Gomer Press, Llandysul

Table of Contents

Acknowledgements

Thanks to everyone who has helped me to research and prepare this book, including Lowell Courtney and David of Lynchpin Tours, Ireland, Frederic Limousin of Novotel, Liz Dale of South West Tourism and Ray Youell at Travel and Tourism Publishing.

As ever I have relied on the support of Debbie and Katie during the writing process. I am grateful to the following organisations who have given permission to use images and copyright material:

ABTA
Association of Independent Tour Operators (AITO)
Association of Train Operating Companies (ATOC)
bmi
County Durham Partnership
Expedia
Foynes Flying Boat Museum, County Limerick
Giant's Causeway visitor centre
Kuoni
Kyle Travel Services
Legoland Windsor
Lynchpin Tours
Northern Ireland Tourist Board
Novotel
Ocean Village
Ray Youell
Shearings Holidays
South West Tourism
Thomas Cook
Thomsonfly
Tourism Ireland
Travmedia
TUI UK/Thomson Holidays
Virgin Trains

Introduction

This book presents 15 case studies of travel and tourism organisations that operate in the UK across different sectors of the industry.

It is intended to support students and tutors of Level 3 BTEC and Nationals, GCE (AS and A2) and Foundation Degree Travel and Tourism courses by providing inside information about real travel and tourism industry organisations.

Each of the 15 case studies, having introduced its subject organisation in broad terms, goes on to outline its history and development to date and to examine its structure and operations, staffing or customer service, finance/funding and marketing. The organisation's likely future path is indicated, and a range of issues to consider is introduced. Each case study concludes with discussion questions, differentiated by level and pertinent to Level 3, AS/A2 or Foundation Degree study.

The travel and tourism industry is dynamic and change can be rapid. This book gives information about each organisation that is up to date at the time of writing and by reflecting on both its recent development and current future issues places all 15 cases in their developing contexts. Travel agent (multiple, miniple and online), long-haul and specialist tour as well as cruise operator, accommodation provider, transport principal (air, rail and coach), visitor attraction and tourism support sectors are all included. The increasingly integrated nature of the travel and tourism industry is reflected within separate case study organisations (Case Study 1 Going Places – part of the Thomas Cook Group – for instance) and head-on by Case Study 15 Thomson/TUI – an integrated mass tourist operator.

The case-by-case material is considered factually and with explanation and comment as appropriate. Information can be used in the study of a wide variety of course modules and units (see matrices on pages vii and viii), including those concerned with the nature and development of travel and tourism, customer service, business operations, marketing and current issues, as well as those dealing with individual sectors such as airlines, accommodation and attractions.

Hard information about real travel and tourism organisations can be difficult or time consuming to obtain for the busy teacher or student. It is hoped that this book will ease the pain to some degree.

How to use this book

This book provides teaching and learning support for GCE, BTEC and National qualifications in Travel and Tourism, as well as for students following Foundation Degree courses.

The 15 up-to-date case studies are each about a real-world travel and tourism organisation. They provide valuable, factual information about individual businesses belonging to the UK travel and tourism industry.

Each case study is structured to a common pattern, featuring the following information sections about its subject organisation:

- Introduction to the organisation;
- Its history/development;
- Structure;
- Operations;
- Staffing/customer service;
- Finance/funding;
- Marketing;
- Future.

In addition, each case includes an Issues section, which highlights current issues facing the organisation and which opens up discussion points for tutors and their students to consider together.

Each of the 15 cases concludes with a set of Discussion Questions. These are differentiated by level (GCE AS and A2, Level 3 and Foundation Degree) and provide opportunities for the reinforcement of learning and pointers towards further research.

Tutors can draw on the case study materials to help teach a wide range of travel and tourism topics. Matrices at the end of this section map out the links between the units of the GCE (AS and A2) and Nationals (including BTEC) Level 3 Specifications of the various awarding bodies (AQA, City and Guilds, Edexcel, OCR and WJEC). Tutors may wish to use a single chapter or case study to exemplify a particular component of the industry (Case Study 5 Ocean Village to illustrate cruising, for example), or else draw on several chapters while delivering a particular topic. Cases 3 (Kuoni), 4 (Lynchpin) and 15 (TUI/Thomson), for example, all concern tour operations, while all 15 case studies feature sections on marketing. The matrices are designed to provide guidance on effective use of the case studies.

Students can also use the book independently to provide supporting information to flesh out topics covered in the class or lecture room and add up-to-date detail to their assignments.

The first of the two matrices below gives some of the main links between the 15 case studies in this book and the GCE AS/A2 and OCR/City and Guilds Level 3 National units that they help to support. Coverage of the BTEC National Level 3 qualification is shown in the second matrix.

Case study			GCE AS/A2				Nationals	
			AQA	Edexcel	OCR	WJEC	C&G	OCR
1	Travel agency multiple	Going Places	1,5	1,10,12	1,3,4,6,15	1,3	301-305	1-6,14
2	Travel agency miniple	Kyle Travel	1,5	1,10,12	1,6,15	1,3	301-305	1-6,14
3	Long-haul tour operator	Kuoni	1,5,13	1,10,12	1,3,4,6,12,13,14,15	1,2,3,7	301-305,308,330	1,3-6,16
4	Specialist tour operator	Lynchpin	1,2,5,13	1,10,12	1,2,6,14,15	1,2,3,4,7	301-305,308	1,3-6,16
5	Cruise operator	Ocean Village	2,5,14	1,7,8,10,12	1,4,6,15	1,3	301-305, 327	1,3-6,10
6	Online travel company	Expedia	1,5,10	1,8,10,12	1,4,6,15	1,3,6	301-305	1,3-6,14
7	Airline	BMI	1,3,5,10	1,8,10,12	1,4,6,15	1,2,3	301-305	1,3-6,17,24
8	Train operator	Virgin Trains	1,5	1,10,12	1,6,15	1,3	301-305	1,3-6,17
9	Coach company	Shearings	1,5	1,10,12	1,6,15	1,3	301-305	1,3-6,17
10	Hotel provider	Novotel	1,2,5,9	1,2,9,10,12	1,2,7,15	1,3,4,7	301-305	1,3-7
11	Natural attraction	The Giant's Causeway	1,5,6,11	1,4,7,8,10,12	1,5,9,15	1,2,3,5,6	301-305,314	1,3-6,20
12	Heritage attraction	Durham Cathedral	1,5,6,11	1,4,10,12	1,5,14,15	1,2,3,5	301-305,312	1,3-6,20,22
13	Built attraction	Legoland Windsor	1,5,6	1,2,4,10,12	1,5,15	1,2,3	301-305,312	1,3-6,20
14	Regional Tourist Board	South West Tourism	1,5,6	1,4,10,12	1,15	1,3,7	301-305,312	1,3-6,20
15	Mass-market tour operator	TUI/Thomson	1,5	1,3,10,12	1,6,15	1,3,7	301-305,308,330	1-6,16

BTEC National units	Case study support
Core units	
Unit 1 Investigating Travel and Tourism	Cases 1-15
Unit 2 The Business of Travel and Tourism	Cases 1-15
Unit 3 The UK as a Destination	Cases 4, 8, 9, 10, 11,12,13,14
Unit 4 Customer Service in Travel and Tourism	Cases 1-15
Specialist units	
Unit 5 Marketing Travel and Tourism Products and Services	Cases 1-15
Unit 6 Preparing for Employment in the Travel and Tourism Industry	Cases 1-15
Unit 7 The European Travel Market	Cases 5, 6, 7, 15
Unit 8 Long-haul Travel Destinations	Cases 3, 6, 7, 15
Unit 9 Retail and Business Travel Operations	Cases 1, 2, 6
Unit 10 Investigating the Cruise Sector	Case 5
Unit 11 Sustainable Tourism Development	Cases 3, 11, 14, 15
Unit 12 Tour Operations	Cases 3, 4, 6, 9, 15
Unit 13 Special Interest Tourism	Cases 3, 4, 14, 15
Unit 14 Roles and Responsibilities of Holiday Representatives	Cases 3, 4, 5, 15
Unit 15 Passenger Transport Issues for the Travel and Tourism Industry	Cases 5, 7, 8, 9,
Unit 16 Events, Conferences and Exhibitions	Cases 10, 13, 14
Unit 17 Tourism in Rural Areas	Cases 11, 14
Unit 18 The Appeal and Importance of UK Visitor Attractions	Cases 11, 12, 13
Unit 19 Hospitality Operations in Travel and Tourism	Case 10
Unit 20 Entertainment for Holidaymakers	Case 5
Unit 21 Work Experience in the Travel and Tourism Industry	Cases 1-15
Unit 22 Residential Study Visit	Cases 1, 2, 3, 6, 11, 12, 13
Unit 24 Handling Air Passengers	Case 7
Unit 25 Working with Children in Holiday Play Settings	Cases 5, 15
Unit 26 Current Issues in Travel and Tourism	Cases 1-15

1

Going Places

– a travel agency multiple

Introduction

Going Places is one of the UK's biggest and best-known high street travel agents. It is a travel agency 'multiple', which means that Going Places has many branches around the country – over 400 in 2007, although this number was as high as 720 in 2002. Like many famous names in the travel and tourism industry, Going Places actually belongs to a larger organisation. It was formerly part of the MyTravel Group, which in turn merged into the Thomas Cook Group of travel companies in 2007. This process of one large organisation owning or controlling different parts of the travel industry is known as 'integration' – the Thomas Cook Group is a vertically-integrated organisation since it owns a wide range of companies at different levels of the chain of distribution in travel and tourism, including travel agencies, tour operators and airlines. As Figure 1.1 indicates, Going Places is now one of Thomas Cook Group's UK and Ireland brands.

History and development

Going Places is a Thomas Cook Group MyTravel brand. Thomas Cook Group is a major integrated travel company within which MyTravel provides package holidays, including short breaks, and flights. Going Places was founded under the name Airtours in the early 1970s.

PRODUCT	BRANDS
Mass market tour operations (upper market range)	**Thomas Cook**
Mass market tour operations (lower market range)	**Airtours**
Tour operations – direct sales	**Direct Holidays**
Scheduled flight packages	**Thomas Cook Signature**
Specialist tour operations	**Club 18-30 / Neilson / Tradewinds**
City breaks	**Bridge / Signature / Cresta**
Ireland tour operations	**Direct Holidays / Panorama / Sunworld**
Travel agency brands	**Thomas Cook / Going Places**
Airline	**Thomas Cook Airlines**

Figure 1.1 *– Thomas Cook Group's UK and Ireland brands*

In 1972 David Crossland, who later founded MyTravel, bought a small Lancashire travel agency business called Pendle Travel Services. Shortly afterwards he acquired another from Albert and Ivy Roberts who had named it AIR Tours, using their own initials in the company name. Crossland kept the Airtours name for the larger business he had now created. During the 1980s Airtours grew to be a major tour operator, launching its own-brand charter airline as it enjoyed continued success in the package holiday market. In the 1990s Airtours bought up other tour operators to further expand its package holiday market share and by the end of the decade had created Going Places – a multiple travel agency chain with, at the time, some 725 outlets, many of which had previously traded under the Hogg Robinson and Pickfords Travel brand names.

In 2002 Airtours re-branded to become MyTravel and its Airtours airline became MyTravel Airways. The Going Places name was retained in the UK for MyTravel's high street travel agent shops, because of the popularity of that brand and the confidence that consumers had in it.

In 2007 MyTravel merged with Thomas Cook Holidays to form an even larger travel company. MyTravel was kept as a name within the overall merged corporation, which was to be called Thomas Cook Group plc. The number of Going Places outlets had by now fallen by more than a third since the brand was created with over 700 outlets in the late 1990s.

Structure

Going Places is a UK travel agency brand belonging to the large international integrated travel company, Thomas Cook Group plc. Thomas Cook Group is organised into five geographically-based divisions:

Figure 1.2 – Going Places is a well-known multiple travel agent

1. **UK and Ireland** – including Going Places, UK tour operations and the MyTravel and Thomas Cook airlines;
2. **Continental Europe** – including Thomas Cook's tour operating businesses in Germany, Austria, France, Belgium, the Netherlands, Hungary and Poland;
3. **Northern Europe** – including MyTravel's businesses in Sweden, Norway, Denmark and Finland;
4. **German airlines** – including the Condor Flugdienst and Condor Berlin airlines, which Thomas Cook operates in Germany;
5. **North America** – including MyTravel's interests in Canada and the USA.

Operations

In 2007 Going Places had 400 high street travel agent shops in the UK. Going Places shops, or stores as it refers to them, stock tour operators' brochures promoting the package holiday products of other Thomas Cook brands (see Figure 1.1 on page 2), as well as those of other tour operators. The sale of Thomas Cook Group products is referred to as in-house selling and accounts for 65% of the travel agent's business.

As with all travel agencies, Going Places staff are involved with both front office and back office operations. Front office operations involve direct customer service including selling products, making reservations, providing advice and handling enquiries. Uniformed travel advisors are on hand to welcome customers and assist them in either browsing the brochures on display or finding extra information. Advisors want to make sales, so they invite potential customers to take a seat when the opportunity arises, since customers who are seated tend to dwell longer and are more likely to become engaged in the booking process. Travel advisor work stations are desks equipped with computers to allow the advisor to search for products to present to customers and to make reservations on their behalf.

Back office operations used to be carried out literally in the back office of a travel agent's shop. In the case of small travel agents like Kyle Travel (see Case Study 2) that largely remains the case, but for multiples like Going Places, back office operations are increasingly undertaken in company offices away from the high street shops in order to streamline processes and save costs. The range of back office operations in a typical travel agency include:

- Accounting;
- Security;
- Stock control;
- Personnel/human resources;
- Marketing.

High street travel agents are a weakening sector of the travel and tourism business. In 2007 there were 5000 travel agent branches in the UK, but there were more than 6000 in 2005. Travel agencies face increasing competition from travel companies that encourage customers to book direct with them over the internet, by 'phone or via digital TV channels. Major travel companies are responding to this threat by reducing their numbers of high street branches and investing in internet and other direct booking ventures.

Going Places has diversified its operations by selling products directly to consumers over the internet as well as through its traditional high street branches. Using the company's website www.goingplaces.co.uk, customers have the option of booking from home at whatever time of day or night suits them, with online travel guidance available. The Going Places website complements the shop window function of its conventional travel agent shops. Customers can visit one of the company's high street stores to collect initial information and brochures for at-home browsing, then make their booking later online from home. Like many travel websites, discounts are offered to generate sales and entice customers to book.

Going Places also operates a call centre. This enables customers to speak to travel advisors directly over the telephone outside of normal high street shop hours. All the tour operator products sold in Going Places shops can also be bought over the telephone, but this method of booking, involving as it does person-to-person contact, does not attract the discounts of making reservations online. Call centres are a growing feature of the UK travel and tourism industry. They make financial sense for the companies concerned, since all their operations and staff can be centred in one location, thereby reducing overhead costs. Call centres can also offer a better service to the public by offering more consistent levels of customer service.

Customer service

Going Places shops' staff that deal directly with the public are called travel advisors. Staff are trained to advise customers on the range of holidays and flights that Going Places sells and to provide information on destinations. From the organisation's point of view the role of Going Places travel advisors is to provide accurate product information to customers using good inter-personal skills so that customers feel at ease and in good hands. Customers are, as a result, more likely to make positive purchase decisions. Such face-to-face sales attract what can be regarded as premium prices, which are not reduced by online discounts.

Brochures are free to take away, and customers need to feel that they able to just walk in to a travel shop and find what they want. Nevertheless, good customer service means that, while callers are allowed such freedom, travel advisors must still be welcoming, checking if there is any further assistance that can be given. Has the customer, for example, been able to collect the brochure s/he wanted? Importantly, so far as the company is concerned, has the customer collected the MyTravel/Thomas Cook brand equivalent brochure? It is also crucial that the potential purchaser of a holiday can act with ease, for example that s/he can easily contact the shop or feel that his/her return visit to make a booking would be welcomed.

Finance/funding

Going Places is part of the Thomas Cook Group, a large transnational (multinational) travel corporation. Thomas Cook is a commercial sector venture whose capital base is provided by its investors. KarstadtQuelle, a German retail company, is the principal and majority shareholder with a 52% holding in 2007, when the company as a whole had a capital value of £2.7 billion. Other major shareholders include financial institutions such as the UK's Standard Life and Legal & General.

Thomas Cook

Figure 1.3 *– Going Places is now part of the Thomas Cook Group*

The expectation of shareholders is that the group as a whole, and constituent businesses within it, will operate at a profit so that dividends can be paid to shareholders and investments made for the future development of the business. In retail travel, however, profitable operations all year round cannot be relied upon, with losses occurring at certain times of the year since demand is low.

Going Places is part of MyTravel, which, along with Thomas Cook, reported profitable year round operations for the three years after 2004 and reduced winter trading losses for the 6 months to April 2007, compared to the same period the year before. The summer of 2006 was particularly warm in the UK. Allied to the summertime staging of that year's football World Cup and heightened terrorism-awareness, the UK travel market was relatively stagnant and Thomas Cook Group's directors were generally satisfied with its overall financial performance. However, there continued to be a decline in the size of the package holiday market (42% of the 2006 UK holiday market compared to 54% in 1998) and in high street travel agency sales, so the decision to close another 45 Going Places shops in the UK was taken.

Marketing

Going Places markets the holidays and travel products of a wide variety of tour operators, including Airtours, Bridge, Cosmos, Eurostar, First Choice, Panorama, Thomson and Thomas Cook. As Figure 1.1 shows, some of these are Thomas Cook Group's own brands, while others are owned and operated by different travel and tourism companies.

Going Places' marketing pitch is that, as a major travel agency multiple, it is a large enough organisation to supply its customers with a wide range of holiday products from which they can choose and on which they can receive advice. However, in many localities, Going Places agencies face competition from small, independent travel agency firms. None of these is anywhere near the size of the Going Places brand, but in any single town centre there is only likely to be one Going Places shop. To the consumer, that is potentially just one among several that may include a local miniple or two (a 'miniple' travel agent is one with a small number of branches in a particular locality). Kyle Travel in Yarm, Cleveland (see Case Study 2) is one such example with just two branches. As a result of such 'little guy' competition, Going Places' self-promotion includes the assertion that it is not too big an organisation to lose sight of the value of the personal touch when advising clients, recognising this as a key selling point of small agencies.

In the marketing mix, place is concerned with the distribution of a business's products and services. Going Places makes its products and services available to its customers in the following ways:

- In its high street Going Places shops;
- Via the Going Places website (www.goingplaces.co.uk);
- Through its call centre.

Bookings made online attract a discount. Holidays and flights provided by tour operators belonging to the MyTravel/Thomas Cook group of companies (Airtours, Aspro, Escapades, Manos and Panorama) attract extra online discounts. This is because of the economies of scale that arise from selling in-house products as well as the need to compete with prices offered by rivals.

To promote Thomas Cook Group own brands, Going Places offers customers a guarantee on price, namely that if they find an Airtours, Aspro, Escapades, Manos or Panorama holiday priced more cheaply by any other travel agent within 24 hours of booking online, Going Places will refund the difference.

Sources of online competition for Going Places are:

- Other travel agency multiples such as TUI (see Case Study 15) who also offer online booking in addition to their shop services;
- Tour operators who sell directly to their customers, for example Direct Holidays and Portland Direct;
- Online travel companies, for example Expedia (Case Study 6) and lastminute.com.

Figure 1.4 illustrates how Going Places' online marketing addresses competition from its internet rivals.

Individual travel providers, such as hotels and transport companies, also market their products online. Their self-packaging customers have probably already chosen not to purchase travel through an agent and may not be seen as lost to Going Places, since they may return to the company in the future book a package holiday. However, self-packaging itself is a growing trend and represents a threat to Going Places and other travel agency businesses in the long term. Self-packaging, when customers put

- **Extra travel information:** We'll also offer you much more than you'll see in the brochures too with our expert online travel guides and advice on a huge range of destinations.

- **Extra time to choose:** We're open 24 hours a day, 7 days a week! So you can book your holiday from the comfort of your own home. If you're looking for other tour operators including First Choice, Thomson, Thomas Cook, Cosmos, Eurostar or city breaks operators visit our stores for great deals. Unfortunately, these tour operators can't be booked online currently. But watch this space as more become available to book online soon!

- **Our Call Centre:** If you'd like to speak to a travel advisor direct over the telephone please call us on 0870 400 1288 and choose option 1. You can book all the tour operators available in our stores by telephone. However, you will not receive any exclusive online discounts.

Figure 1.4 *– Benefits of booking online with Going Places*

together their own holidays and book direct (usually over the internet), is also known as 'dynamic packaging'.

Future

The future of the high street travel agent remains uncertain although the sector's role is likely to decline further in a UK travel market which overall is regarded by Thomas Cook Group as "likely to remain challenging" into at least the near future. In June 2007 Thomas Cook Group announced that the main brand name used by its UK travel agent shops would be Thomas Cook, but that Going Places would remain the name for existing stores that were profitable and where there was another Thomas Cook travel agency in the same town.

Dynamic packaging is likely to grow more in the near future. Going Places' shops plan to respond by selling a flexible mix or products – traditional charter holidays, flight-only deals (using charter, scheduled and more often low-cost airlines) and accommodation-only breaks for beach as well as city destinations.

Going Places' management sees growth in online booking as set to continue into the future. They have researched how customers progress through their online journeys so the Going Places website can be developed to allow easy access to as much accurate information as possible.

Social networking via the internet is a future opportunity for travel agents like Going Places. Many Going Places customers decide about their next holiday because of what other people have recommended. Going Places plans to increase social networking content including consumer hotel reviews, blogs and video submissions on its websites.

Issues to consider

1. The future of high street travel agents is uncertain in the long term. The bulk of the conventional travel agents' market was retailing package holidays. However, package holidays' share of the UK holidays market has fallen to less than half. There are also other ways to book – via call centres and on the internet. In 2007 there were 5000 high street travel agent branches left. By 2012 there may only be 2000.

   CONSIDER: Where else retail travel agents such as Going Places can establish outlets and thereby increase sales.

2. The continued growth of the Internet has had great impacts on the travel agency sector. Business has been lost to online bookers and travel agents have had to adapt to keep up with internet developments.

   CONSIDER: How retail travel agents like Going Places have changed their practices in order to counter the growth of the internet.

3. Going Places was already integrated into MyTravel when it merged with Thomas Cook in 2007.

CONSIDER: The advantages and disadvantages to travel companies of continued integration.

4. About two-thirds of the holidays sold by Going Places shops are Thomas Cook Group products.

CONSIDER: Whether it would be to Going Places' advantage for it to sell exclusively Thomas Cook products.

5. The Going Places' brand name is being retained in towns where a Thomas Cook travel shop already exists.

CONSIDER: The likely effects of the competition between retail travel agents in a town where this is the case.

6. Employment opportunities in travel agencies are declining – more than 2000 jobs were threatened by the 2007 merger of MyTravel and Thomas Cook.

CONSIDER: The implications for young people planning a career in retail travel.

7. There is some evidence to suggest that the recent trend of increased online booking is slowing down.

CONSIDER: Is there a limit to what will be booked online?

8. Social networking on the internet has expanded a great deal and shows every sign of continuing to do so. Going Places customers' holiday choices are heavily influenced by other people's travel experiences.

CONSIDER: The marketing opportunities that online social networking offers retail travel agents such as Going Places.

Discussion questions

(differentiated by level)

1. Apply AIDA analysis (attention, interest, desire, action) to a Going Places or other retail travel agency shop (Level3/GCE AS).

2. Describe and evaluate the fitness for purpose of a travel advisor's work station. Use your own observations or experience of a Going Places or similar travel agency premises to help you (Level 3/GCE A2).

3. How should the managers of a Going Places travel agency and a Thomas Cook travel agent in the same town interact? (GCE A2/ Foundation Degree).

4. Discuss the implications for a travel company's management and shareholders of merging with a competitor (Foundation Degree).

2

Kyle Travel

– a travel agency miniple

Introduction

Kyle Travel is a small travel agency with two shops in the Tees Valley in North East England. One of the shops is in the commuter town of Yarm, Cleveland (see Figure 2.1) and the other is in Barnard Castle, a market town in County Durham.

Figure 2.1 – *Kyle Travel*

The business is a 'miniple'. Travel agency miniples are small to medium-sized companies with few rather than many branches, often clustered in a particular geographical region. Despite the contraction and horizontal integration of the travel agency sector in recent years, miniples like Kyle Travel continue to trade profitably, often in city suburbs and rural towns, providing a personalised service to many loyal customers.

Development

Kyle Travel Services, to give the business its full name, was established by Eddie Kyle in Yarm in 1982. It has grown in branch terms only to the extent of having a second shop in Barnard Castle.

Kyle Travel is of a similar size to the Airtours business established by David Crossland in Lancashire in 1972. That eventually grew into the major integrated travel company MyTravel, including the travel agent multiple Going Places (see Case Study 1). Such growth is not the ambition of Kyle Travel for whom smallness of size, personal attention and high local reputation are key selling points.

Kyle Travel is a member of AITO – the Association of Independent Tour Operators, in the Specialist Travel Agent category. AITO membership enables Kyle Travel to market holidays packaged by fellow AITO members who are specialist tour operators. These are products which are often not available from mainstream travel agents. Multiples like Going Places promote in-house brands rather than the products of small, independent operators. Going Places is a Thomas Cook Group brand – 65% of Going Places sales are of Thomas Cook Group holidays and travel products.

***Figure 2.2** – Kyle Travel is a member of AITO*

Kyle Travel specialises in travel to Australia and the USA, plus cruising holidays worldwide. However, this does not mean that these are the only markets in which the firm deals. Kyle Travel sells a broad range of holiday and travel products to destinations around the world and in specialist markets, including skiing and wine tasting tours. It also acts as a ticket agent for transport providers such as the local, County Durham-based Classic Coaches.

Structure

Kyle Travel has two retail outlets and an internet website www.kyletravel.co.uk. Mr Eddie Kyle is the founder and proprietor. As well as being a member of AITO, Kyle Travel also belongs to Worldchoice.

Established in 1976, Worldchoice is a consortium of more than 800 independent UK leisure travel agents. Membership means Kyle Travel can compete with travel agency multiples like Going Places on price. This is because of economies of scale. The bargaining power of a co-operative association like Worldchoice means that deals can be struck with tour operators and principals (airlines, hotel companies, etc.) to provide their holidays at similar prices to the large travel agent chains, while still retaining sufficient margins to trade profitably.

Membership of both AITO and Worldchoice enables Kyle Travel to maintain its independent, small business, 2-branch structure in a market where otherwise such a relatively tiny enterprise would not be able to compete. Co-operative interaction with other SMEs (small to medium-sized enterprises) in the travel and tourism industry is an important factor in the continued existence of travel agency miniples. This is especially so when the high street travel agent sector as a whole is in relative decline, with the total number of branches forecast to more than halve between 2007 and 2012.

Operations

Through its two shops, and via its website, Kyle Travel provides a wide range of travel products and services, including package holidays, cruises and short breaks, air, rail and coach travel tickets, car hire, hotel bookings and travel insurance.

Kyle Travel's operations are diverse. As well as selling the package holiday, short-break and cruise products of tour operators, Kyle's travel consultants also arrange events and itineraries including:

- Weddings and honeymoons;
- Party trips such as stag and hen nights;
- Tailor-made itineraries, including safaris and other long-haul tours, for individuals and groups;
- Luxury and theatre breaks in the UK and overseas, including tickets for major events and attractions;
- Bargain flights, including round-the-world air tickets;
- Activity-based holidays, including skiing, golfing and diving;
- Exclusive UK coach holidays.

Kyle Travel also supplies support services to its customers, including arranging airport car parking, lounge access and hotel bookings, travel insurance, foreign currency, passports and visas.

Providing advice to customers about its various products and services, and making bookings on their behalf, are Kyle Travel's 'front office', or 'front of house' operations. These are the ones that customers experience when visiting the shops. The website www.kyletravel.co.uk provides similar functions online. The home page greets customers and makes it immediately possible to search and book holidays. Other services can be accessed via links to other pages of the website – for example the hyperlinked tickets and attractions page. The front office operations of handling credit and debit card payments and promoting the products that are for sale are also enabled and customers are able to access legal information about terms and conditions. To facilitate Kyle Travel's provision of information to its customers, the website provides telephone and e-mail contacts.

'Back office' operations take place behind the scenes. Kyle Travel's main office is at its Yarm shop. Here, the full range of management functions are carried out, for example management of people (human resources, customer data and health and safety), stock (brochures), marketing and publicity, development (including the website) and finance (accounts, forecasts).

Customer service

The staff of Kyle Travel are travel consultants. Key selling points for a travel agency miniple are the experience of its staff and the consequent knowledge and expertise they are able to bring to bear when matching a product or destination to the customer's needs.

Kyle Travel is keen to promote the broad varied experience of its travel consultants in specialist markets, including adventure tourism, camping holidays, rail tours, sailing and winter sports. To keep up to date and broaden their experience, staff are encouraged to take part in familiarisation trips that are offered by tour operators and principals, in order to broaden and deepen their product knowledge.

Typical of a small, independent travel company (see Case Study 4 on Lynchpin for a tour operator comparison), Kyle Travel concentrates on providing a personal service that is as closely tailored as is possible to customers' specific needs. Repeat business and personal recommendations are very important to the continued profitability of the business, so the personal touch of all consultants is vital.

Finance and marketing

Kyle Travel is a small business in the commercial sector. Financially, it depends in the end upon trading surpluses to fund its continuation. Marketing is its lifeblood – without marketing there would be no trade, and no surplus. So, for Kyle Travel, finance and marketing are inextricably linked.

Product, price, place and promotion are the ingredients in the marketing mix. Kyle Travel's products are, of course, the holidays, travel tickets and ancillary services (such as travel insurance and airport parking) that it sells. To survive in a declining travel agency sector, with travel agent multiples as competitors, Kyle Travel has tailored its product range, partly through its membership of AITO, towards specialist and long-haul markets, to offer products that are distinct from those of mainstream agents like Going Places and Thomson.

Kyle Travel has built up a very good local reputation in the Tees Valley area for excellent customer service delivered through the personal attention of its travel consultants. Service quality is a major part of Kyle Travel customers' purchase and, therefore, an important part of the company's 'product offering'.

Price and promotion are closely linked to Kyle Travel's Worldchoice and AITO memberships. Being a part of the Worldchoice consortium of over 800 travel agents allows Kyle Travel to price products as competitively as its travel agency multiple rivals. The ability to use both AITO and ABTA (Association of British Travel Agents) logos in its promotional materials, including on the Kyle Travel website, is a major part of the company promoting itself as a small travel agency in which the first-time customer can have complete confidence.

Figure 2.3
Kyle Travel is a member of ABTA

'Place' in the marketing mix refers to the channels of distribution through which a business makes its products available to its customers. In Kyle Travel's case, these vehicles are its two shops and its website. Competing travel agents in the immediate localities of the shops are few, although there is a Thomson branch in Yarm and Travelcare have a shop in Barnard Castle. In both towns, reputation is key to Kyle Travel's appeal. Small towns are places where a higher proportion of people know each other than is generally the case in cities. It is with this in mind that Kyle Travel promotes its personally-delivered customer service as 'discreet'.

Future

The travel agency high street shop sector is in a period of rapid change, with many fewer outlets than there used to be – the number of UK travel agency branches fell by more than 1000 between 2005 and 2007. This downward trend is expected to continue. However, despite this position, travel agent miniples such as Kyle Travel continue to exist despite the marketing power of major multiples like the Thomas Cook/Going Places and Thomson/TUI chains (Case Studies 1 and 15).

In part, the likely continuation of miniples into the future is down to the personalised service they are able to deliver and to their consequent high local reputations. This is true of Kyle Travel. It also arises from continued membership of larger groupings such as Worldchoice (which confers some of the market muscle larger organisations are able to flex) and AITO.

From Kyle Travel's perspective, the future extrapolation of trends that have recently affected AITO members is encouraging. AITO member travel agents experienced a 60% rise in bookings in 2006, reflecting a desire on the part of the travelling public for more adventure and specialist interest tourism. Since 70% of business is from repeat bookings, this positive outlook looks likely to continue, at least in the short-term. While AITO travel agents, like the whole sector, have seen package holiday sale volumes fall, demand for 'dynamic packaging', when customers use the internet to put together their own holidays, is continuing to rise year-on-year. Given other trends, such as the continued growth of budget airlines and rising demand for long-haul destinations, prospects look good for AITO member travel agents like Kyle Travel who are able to sell independent specialist tour operator products, either as individual travel components or as part of tailor-made packages.

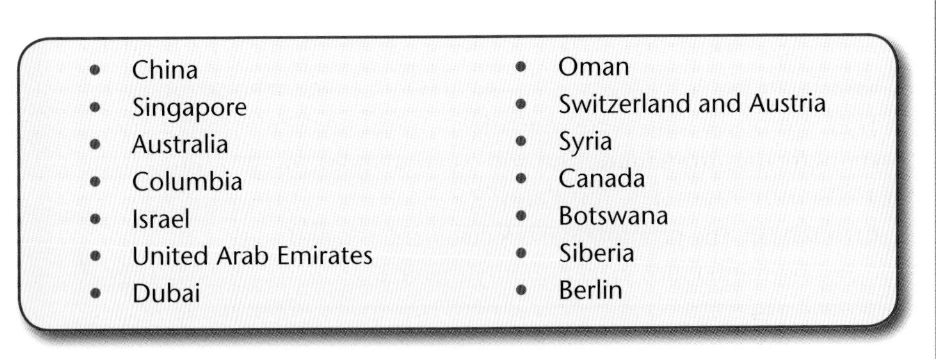

- China
- Singapore
- Australia
- Columbia
- Israel
- United Arab Emirates
- Dubai
- Oman
- Switzerland and Austria
- Syria
- Canada
- Botswana
- Siberia
- Berlin

***Figure 2.4** – ABTA's 'hot destinations' for 2008*

Destinations that ABTA predicts will show increased volumes in 2008 are shown in Figure 2.4. Kyle Travel is hoping to capitalise on the increased demand for long-haul travel indicated in this forecast.

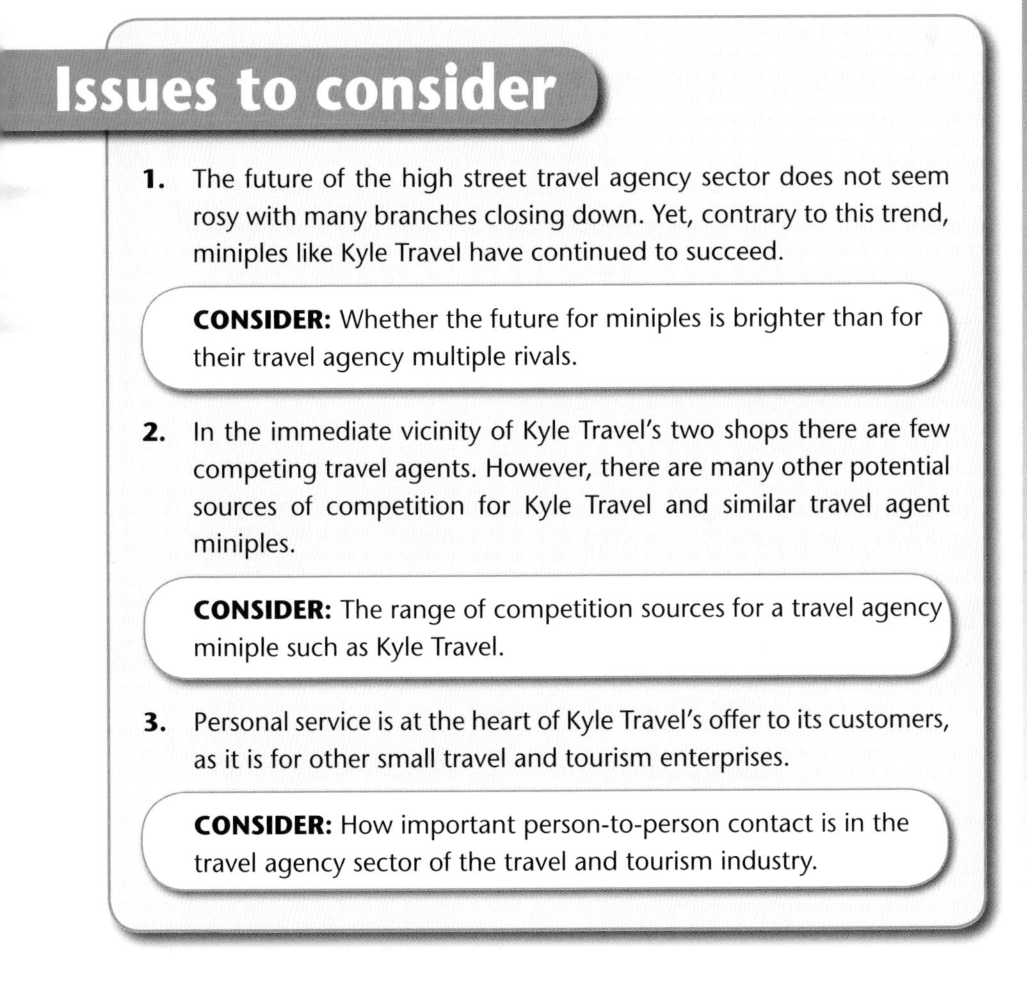

Issues to consider

1. The future of the high street travel agency sector does not seem rosy with many branches closing down. Yet, contrary to this trend, miniples like Kyle Travel have continued to succeed.

   CONSIDER: Whether the future for miniples is brighter than for their travel agency multiple rivals.

2. In the immediate vicinity of Kyle Travel's two shops there are few competing travel agents. However, there are many other potential sources of competition for Kyle Travel and similar travel agent miniples.

   CONSIDER: The range of competition sources for a travel agency miniple such as Kyle Travel.

3. Personal service is at the heart of Kyle Travel's offer to its customers, as it is for other small travel and tourism enterprises.

   CONSIDER: How important person-to-person contact is in the travel agency sector of the travel and tourism industry.

4. Kyle Travel publicity features ABTA, AITO and Worldchoice logos. They are organisations to which Kyle Travel belongs in order to strengthen its market position and promote sales.

CONSIDER: The promotional effectiveness of Kyle Travel featuring these logos in its publicity materials.

5. 'Dynamic packaging' is increasingly popular with customers.

CONSIDER: Whether continued growth in dynamic packaging is likely to benefit independent retail travel agents.

6. Kyle Travel offers a wide variety of travel services and specialist holidays, often supplied by AITO member tour operators.

CONSIDER: How a travel agency miniple such as Kyle Travel can differentiate its product range from that of a typical travel agency multiple.

Discussion questions

(differentiated by level)

1. What is the range of 'back office' operations needed to support a retail travel website such as that of Kyle Travel? (Level 3/GCE AS).

2. a) Evaluate the threats to Kyle Travel as a business.
   b) Analyse the ways in which Kyle Travel has addressed these threats. (Level3/GCE A2).

3. Devise a forward-looking strategy for Kyle Travel as a business in the short to medium term (Foundation Degree).

Kuoni

– a long-haul tour operator

Introduction

Kuoni is an international tour operating company. Although it operates some short-haul holidays, Kuoni is perhaps best known in the UK as a long-haul and specialist tour operator. Figure 3.1 (on page 22) lists the Kuoni brochures available in the UK marketplace in 2007-8.

History and development

Kuoni was founded by Alfred Kuoni in Switzerland in 1906 when he added a travel agency to the family freight transport business.

Since 1966, Kuoni has been a major long-haul tour operator in the UK market. More recently it has diversified into 'niche markets' by acquiring previously independent specialist tour operator businesses. These have included Voyages Jules Verne, Travel Collection and Sport Abroad – brands which continue to operate autonomously within the wider Kuoni Group. Kuoni UK underwent a major restructuring in 2006-7 (its centenary year) and broadened its product range by purchasing two upmarket touring holiday brands – Journeys of Distinction and Kirker Holidays. This was in line with Kuoni's current strategy of focusing on high quality travel products.

Long-haul	Short-haul	Specialist/niche
Worldwide World Class *luxury long-haul* Tropical Sun *3-star* Southern Africa Dubai Sri Lanka China Indo-China Seychelles Morocco Florida Africa and Indian Ocean Egypt America and Canada Australia, New Zealand and South Pacific	Swiss Summer Italy World Class Europe	Weddings Wisden Cricket Supporters Tours H2O *water-centred* Sandals *Sandals all-incusives* Beaches *Beaches all-incusives* Taj Taj *hotels* Limited Editions Lakes and Mountains Sport Abroad: Rugby Sport Abroad: Motorsport Sport Abroad: Cricket Snow Selections *holidays with Emirates flights*

***Figure 3.1** – Kuoni's product range in the UK*

Figure 3.2 charts the major milestones in Kuoni's UK history and development.

Structure

Figure 3.3 shows Kuoni's organisational structure. Kuoni Travel Holdings Ltd is the Kuoni Group parent company. The company put a new structure into effect in 2007. This is a structure which has three strategic business divisions (SBDs):

- 'Style' – upper market range branded products, including Kuoni own-name holidays;
- 'Smart' – lower cost holidays;
- Destinations – local, in-destination operations.

1966	Kuoni UK established
1969	Launch of packaged safari and beach holidays in East Africa
1970	First package charters to the Far East
1972	Sri Lanka and Thailand packages
1974	Expanded into the Caribbean through take-over of competitor Houlders World Holidays
1976	Opens up the Brazil market to UK package tourists
1979	USA destination expansion
1980	Introduces lower cost long-haul holidays (Kuoni3) using 3-star hotels
1981	Summer Swiss holidays introduced
1983	Ski holidays to Switzerland added
1986	Launch of the Limited Editions brochure – short-term availability flights and hotels
1987	Maldives packages begun
1988	Launches KUDOS Viewdata reservations system for travel agents
1991	Australia launch
1992	Reservations system linked to Galileo, the scheduled airlines computer reservations system
1997	Established call centre with 50 extra sales staff
1998	Acquires the Voyages Jules Verne brand
2000	Launches World Class brochure of luxury long-haul holidays
2001	Website expanded to enable consumer self-packaging online
2002	Further website expansion with specialist activity section
2004	First Families brochure
2005	Launch of single destination brochures, such as Morocco

Figure 3.2 *– Milestones in Kuoni's history and development*

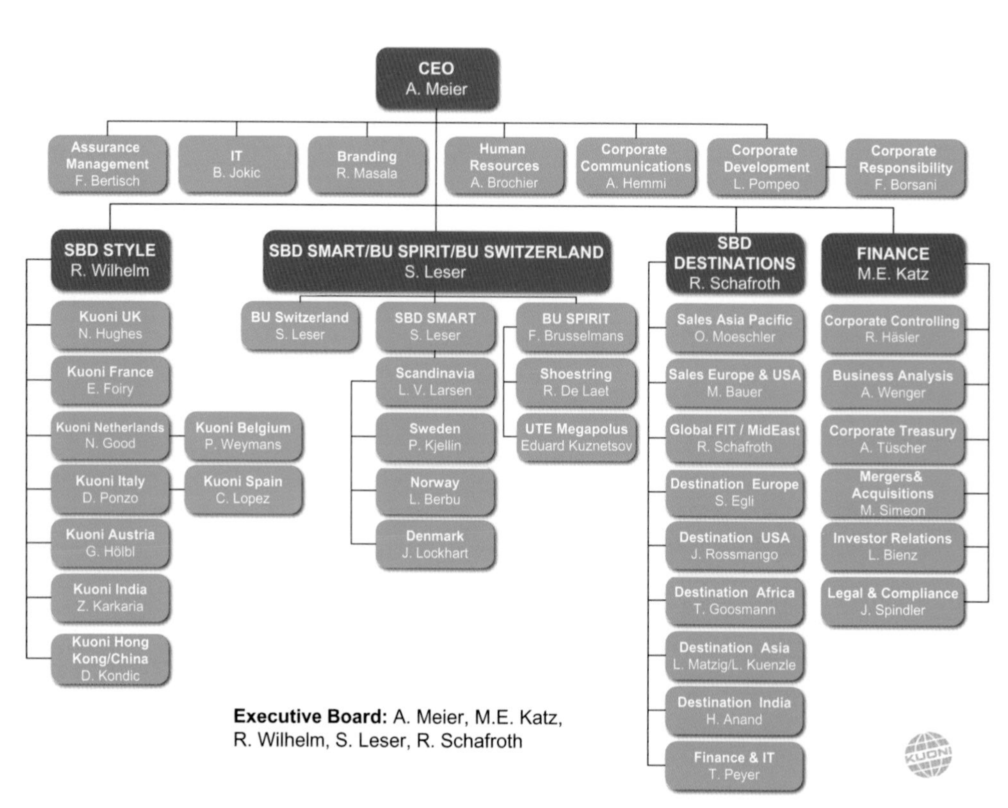

Figure 3.3 *– Kuoni's organisational structure*

Kuoni Group's Executive Board consists of the Chief Executive Officer (CEO), Chief Finance Officer and the three SBD Heads. The CEO directly oversees the management of a range of corporate functions, including the branding and marketing department, which works on developing Kuoni's range of brands in partnership with the SBDs.

The Style SBD includes those Kuoni Group operations that focus on high quality, premium holiday products. The Kuoni own-name brand and all the group's other specialist brands are also in this division. The Kuoni UK business unit became part of the 'Style' SBD as a result of the 2007 restructuring.

'Smart' SBD is concerned with those Kuoni products that aim at the budget end of the market. This includes some brands not marketed in the UK, for example Apollo, Helvetic Tours, Reisen Netto and Kuoni's two airlines, Edelweiss Air and Novair. The products of the 'Smart' division are currently sold mainly through travel agents, but more direct consumer sales via the internet are planned. The special business unit (BU) 'Spirit' is responsible for developing new ideas. Structurally, it is part of the 'Smart' SBD.

SBD 'Destinations' covers the Kuoni Group's in-destination operations including MICE (meetings, incentives, conferences and events), special tours and sports events. The 'Destinations' division provides services for other international tour operators, for travel agents and for conference organisers, as well as for Kuoni's own tour operating brands.

Kuoni owns a range of specialist brands which trade in the UK as autonomous businesses. These include:

- Kuoni Sport Abroad – a specialist sports brand offering supporters tours to major sporting events, such as cricket, rugby, motor sport, horse racing, fishing and golf;
- The Travel Collection – operating tours that are designed to provide unusual travel experiences;
- Voyages Jules Verne – specialising in small group travel to destinations which have special cultural appeal, for example Egypt, China and Italy;
- Journeys of Distinction – upmarket, escorted tours to long-haul destinations.

Operations

Kuoni operates travel branches based in over 30 countries in Europe, Asia, Africa and North America. The two key fields in which it operates are:

1. Leisure travel (holidays);
2. Destination management (in-destination operations).

Leisure Travel

Kuoni's core operations are to provide personal advice on holidays, to devise holiday products and to distribute these through travel agents, call centres and via the internet. As a tour operating company, Kuoni organises both package and tailor-made holidays. This includes selecting destinations, planning products based on market trends and completing contracting agreements either with agents or directly with local transport, accommodation and support service providers in holiday destinations. The next stage of the operation is to distribute these holiday products for sale to customers.

Destination Management

Kuoni's destination management operations include organising, and advising customers on, seminars, congresses, special interest and incentive tours, and sports events. Arrangements are made for groups, often from the corporate sector, and for individual travellers. Kuoni also sells its destination management services to other international tour operators.

Kuoni's Destination Management division has five business units (BUs) within it, as Figure 3.3 on page 24 indicates. These are based on geographical regions of the world:

- Destination Management Europe;
- Destination Management USA;
- Destination Management India;
- Destination Management Africa;
- Destination Management Asia.

Kuoni's Destination Management SBD has fourteen offices in Europe, six in North America, ten in India, three in Africa and nineteen in Asia. Destination Management Europe concentrates on serving customers who are visiting Europe from Asia, the Middle East, India and North America. The USA office deals with customers from Europe, Asia and South America, while the offices in Asia and Africa are concerned primarily with European visitors.

Staffing

Despite major restructuring in 2006-7, Kuoni has maintained its previous level of staffing. Altogether, Kuoni employs more than 7,500 staff in its 300 offices worldwide. This includes 1500 employees in its destination management operations around the world.

Ownership and finance

Kuoni UK is owned by Kuoni Travel Holdings Ltd, a transnational corporation with its headquarters in Zurich in Switzerland. Figure 3.3 on page 24 shows the Kuoni Group's organisational structure. Kuoni's global turnover in 2006 was over 4000 billion Swiss Francs. Leisure travel operations accounted for 80% of this, the remainder coming from its in-destination activities. The Group's turnover showed a 15% increase in the first half of 2007, when compared to the same period in 2006.

***Figure 3.4** – the Kuoni logo*

Marketing

Marketing is used to bring about the sale of Kuoni's products by blending product, price, place and promotion – the four ingredients in the marketing mix. The leisure travel products that account for 80% of Kuoni's turnover are promoted in the UK principally via its varied suite of brochures (see Figure 3.1) and its UK website www.kuoni.co.uk. In 2007, Kuoni UK's brochure front covers carried the statement "Voted by travel agents 'best long-haul tour operator' for 24 years". Together with the restrained design of these covers, this helped convey a subliminal marketing message of quality, rather than cheapness (see Figure 3.5).

***Figure 3.5** – The Kuoni weddings brochure*

Kuoni's marketing aims to attract customers from a wide spectrum of interest groups. Varying brochure concepts is one strategy the organisation uses to this end. Market segments of customers looking for luxury holidays, lower priced 3-star holidays, sports-based holidays and holidays in particular destinations are among those targeted. Partnerships with other iconic travel organisations such as Sandals – providers of all-inclusive resorts in the Caribbean – are overtly promoted with the aim of widening the customer base still further. The Kuoni Beaches brochure is companion to the Sandals product – Beaches resorts are Sandals-owned. The Beaches brand includes families in its target market segment, while Sandals itself deliberately limits its appeal to couples.

Kuoni's call centres add further breadth to the marketing drive, within the place component of the marketing mix, by adding variety to the range of distribution channels used. Specialist brochures, such as the one shown in Figure 3.5, each invite callers to use different telephone numbers 'for expert advice', six or seven days a week. Brochures can be ordered via another dedicated telephone line or, as e-brochures via the internet site. In addition to receiving face-to-face service from a travel agent, UK customers are welcome at Kuoni's head office in Dorking, Surrey (see Figure 3.6) and at branches in London and Manchester.

***Figure 3.6** – Kuoni's UK head office*

Future

Kuoni aims to be the world's best and most successful tourist travel company. It won the 'World's Leading Tour Operator' award in 2006 (for the eighth time) and has been voted 'Best Long-haul Tour Operator' by UK travel agents for 24 years (to 2007).

To maintain such a level of performance into the future Kuoni exhorts its staff to make it different, in the eyes of customers, from other tour operators by delivering customer service 'with passion'. At the same time, it is on-going company policy to use the latest available technology.

A sign of Kuoni's future marketing strategy is the opening by Kuoni of new-style, direct-sale travel outlets for its products in some leading European cities. These outlets have lounge areas with travel libraries, touch-screen monitors for exploring Kuoni's leisure travel products and, in some cases, café-bars. Paris, Strasbourg and Toulouse in France, Gothenburg in Sweden and Zurich in Switzerland are the first cities where Kuoni has introduced these outlets.

In the UK, 2006 was a difficult year for the travel and tourism industry. A terrorist attack on London's Heathrow Airport was averted, but the associated publicity damaged consumer confidence and greater security measures complicated airport procedures for passengers. Furthermore, it was, by UK standards, an unusually warm summer that year. All in all, demand for Kuoni's products declined, as it did for those of other organisations. Kuoni UK's EBIT (earnings before interest and tax) figure showed a 10% year-on-year fall. Kuoni's United Kingdom strategic business unit (SBU) responded to these changed market conditions by restructuring its business for the future. It revised and expanded its portfolio of holiday products (see Figure 3.1) and began to put a stronger focus on high quality travel products by acquiring the Journeys of Distinction and Kirker Holidays brands. The future direction of Kuoni in the UK is set to be an upmarket provider, with high quality and luxury tours to the fore.

Increased awareness by the travelling public, and by governments, of the environmental and social impacts of tourism has prompted tour operators like Kuoni to develop responsible tourism policies. Kuoni's future responsible tourism policy is to:

- Constantly review operations to check that they are socially and environmentally sustainable;
- Contribute positively to the economies of destinations, while, at the same time, trying to minimise negative impacts on the environment and on local cultures;
- Co-operate with local communities by purchasing local products and using locally available skills;
- Respect the natural and cultural heritages of destinations;
- Use the natural resources of destinations, including the land itself and energy and water supplies, responsibly;
- Update staff and customers on Kuoni's responsible tourism policy and actively encourage them to care for the environment and to keep negative impacts minimal.

Issues to consider

1. Kuoni is a long-haul tour operator. Long-haul travel involves air travel. There is rising concern from the public, from the media and from governments about its impact on the atmosphere. In particular, anxieties are expressed about air travel's contribution to global warming. Kuoni works with the organisation Climate Care to offset the carbon dioxide emissions of the planes its customers use. This is done by funding projects to develop renewable energy supplies, encourage energy efficiency and restore areas of damaged forest in various parts of the world, for example the restoration of tropical rain forest in the Kibale National Park in Uganda.

CONSIDER: The extent to which it is the responsibility of tour operators like Kuoni to address climate change.

2. Many long-haul travel destinations are in the less economically developed world (LEDW). The social sustainability of tourism to these places is another growing concern. Kuoni has been involved in a number of projects to raise money to improve the standard of living of children in tourist receiving areas of the LEDW. An example was money the company gave in 2004 to the charity SOS

Children's Villages to provide teaching aids for a village school in Vietnam.

CONSIDER: How tour operators can promote positive social impacts in destinations.

3. Kuoni's strategy in the UK is to increasingly target special interest groups towards the upper end of the market.

CONSIDER: The extent to which this is a significant change in direction and the reasons behind it.

4. Kuoni has not traditionally run its own travel agent shops, although customers are welcomed at its offices. Recently, Kuoni has opened direct sales outlets in selected European cities.

CONSIDER: The effectiveness of travel outlets and shops in the digital age.

5. Kuoni produces over 20 different brochures for the UK market. The intention is to widen the company's appeal to as many interest groups as possible.

CONSIDER: The degree of specialism needed for brochures that are aimed at the premium end of the leisure travel market.

6. Although best known in the UK as a long-haul tour operator, Kuoni also operates some short-haul holidays.

CONSIDER: The potential for Kuoni to expand this part of its business.

7. About one fifth of Kuoni's 2006 turnover came from its destination management activities, largely targeted at the corporate market and including services to other tour operators.

CONSIDER: The extent to which Kuoni's destination management activities should remain part of the company's future strategy.

Discussion questions

(differentiated by level)

1. Why are long-haul operators such as Kuoni especially concerned about responsible tourism issues? (Level 3/GCE AS).

2. Kuoni targets a wide range of customer types. Explain who are not Kuoni target market cutomers? (Level 3/GCE A2).

3. Analyse how Kuoni uses the four elements of the marketing mix to broaden its customer base (Level 3/GCE A2).

4. Before 2007, Kuoni had a geographically-based structure. Then the company changed to one based on three strategic business divisions (SBDs). Suggest potential benefits to Kuoni's business of this change (Foundation Degree).

4

Lynchpin Tours

– a specialist, independent tour operator

Introduction

Lynchpin is a small tour operating company, owned and managed by two business partners and based in Portrush, County Antrim, Northern Ireland. Lynchpin specialises in putting together tour itineraries that are tailor-made to meet the needs of small groups of incoming visitors to Ireland. Although Lynchpin's office is in Northern Ireland, most of its tours are based in the Republic of Ireland.

The company offers customised, guided tours, using coaches and executive minibuses depending on the size of the groups. It aims to provide customers with the chance to see Ireland while enjoying their own particular special interest. Lynchpin caters for a wide range of special interests, including:

- Genealogy (family-history);
- Golf;
- Food and drink;
- Mystic Ireland.

Lynchpin offers sample itineraries (see Figure 4.1), but the partners prefer to work with clients to build tours that suit their specific, personal needs.

Mystic Ireland: outline itinerary

DAY 1: Accommodation: Ashling Hotel, Dublin
Arrive Dublin Airport where our Tour Manager will be waiting to greet you and to escort you onto our luxury coach which is yours for the entire duration of the trip. Half day city tour of Dublin.

DAY 2: TARA — Seat of the ancient High Kings of Ireland Accommodation: Armagh City Hotel
Depart Dublin to travel to Tara. From here to Mellifont, the first Cistercian Abbey in Ireland. Armagh.

DAY 3: ARMAGH Accommodation: Carlton Hotel, Belleek
After breakfast, visit Armagh then west to the village of Belleek, home to the famous pottery.

DAY 4: SLIGO, ROSCOMMON
Today we turn south to the heartland of Ireland and places other tours pass by. Crevykeel Court Tomb. Strokestown House in Co. Roscommon - one of Ireland's least known "great houses": Carefully managed by John O'Driscoll and his team, Strokestown has the last surviving Georgian kitchen in the country plus an excellent famine museum. Highly recommended yet relatively unknown.

We finish the day on the river Shannon at Athlone, the true heart of Ireland.

DAY 5: CLONMACNOISE, CONNAUGHT, AND HAUNTED CASTLES Meals: Breakfast, Dinner Accommodation: Three Star Dundrum House and Leisure Centre
Leaving Athlone, we follow the Shannon to the ancient monastic site of Clonmacnoise. Its location tells you why and how such a large monastic site developed here: it was the main crossing point into the western province of Connaught. It has a spectacular setting on the river and, given a little peace, you can easily be transported back 1000 years. From there we keep south and arrive in the neat town of Birr and its castle and demesne. Still home to Lord and Lady Rosse, Birr Castle has a delightful garden with its historic telescope.

From there we go to one of the highlights of this tour — Ireland's most haunted castle at Leap (pronounced "Lep".) Bob Curran will be only too happy to regale you with tales of horror and haunting! We then go to the rock of Dunamas and finish off the day at the three star Dundrum House near Cashel.

DAY 6: CORK AND KERRY Meals: Breakfast, Dinner Accommodation: Three Star Gleann Fia Guest House in Killarney
After breakfast, on to the main Cork road and bypass the city through the Jack Lynch tunnel, named after a sportsman who won all Ireland football and hurling medals and who went on to become Taoiseach (Prime Minister) in the 1970s. First call is at the Cobh (pronounced "Cove") Heritage Centre, a very popular visitor attraction with its story of the Great Hunger, the Titanic and the Lusitania — aren't you glad you came by air?
From Cobh we turn west again on the road to Kerry (known as "The Kingdom") via Macroom and visit the ruined castle of Carrickphouka. Our overnight is in the three star Gleann Fia guest house in Killarney — bed and breakfast.

DAY 7: WESTERN ADVENTURE Meals: Breakfast, Dinner at Bunratty Castle Banquet Accommodation: Bunratty Guest House
Leaving Killarney, we head to the coast to see the ruins of Ardfert cathedral. As you watch the Atlantic rolling in, it is a sobering thought that there is nothing but sea between you and Cape Cod. You might even hum a verse of "Nearer, my Cod, to Thee..." in memory of the 1500 souls lost on the Titanic. Turning towards Limerick, we call at the excellent Writers' Museum in Listowel, before crossing the Shannon for the last time at Limerick and heading for our final night in family run guest houses in Bunratty. The final dinner will be at the Bunratty Castle banquet, a splendid piece of mock medieval nonsense which is great fun.

DAY 8: DEPARTURE
Short morning transfer from Bunratty to Shannon airport for your flight home.

Figure 4.1 *– A sample itinerary from Lynchpin Tours*

History and development

Lynchpin's two partners, David and Lowell (see Figure 4.2), established the business in 1997. Each had followed a previous, professional career. David was a bank manager and Lowell had been a teacher. As a result, both had good people-handling skills, as well as relevant expertise in finance and in languages. Both are Irish. When they planned their business they agreed that they would enjoy bringing their knowledge and passion for Ireland to visitors. David and Lowell intended that Lynchpin would bring them some financial return and even greater job satisfaction.

Since 1997 the partners have gradually built up trade in the tours. They have done so by establishing a network of accommodation and transport suppliers across Ireland, by establishing a high reputation among clients for quality and personal service, and by taking advantage of opportunities afforded by the internet to attract business from overseas, most notably the USA.

Figure 4.2 *– Lynchpin's business partners*

The golf tour has become one of Lynchpin's most successful tour products. Genealogy tours arise from the growing demand for "roots tourism" – the interest, largely among grey-market tourists, in visiting the places from which their ancestors came and in which they may still have relatives. Irish-American empty-nesters (adults whose children have grown up and left home) are an important target market for Lynchpin. Culinary tourism and interest in visiting sites associated with the myths and legends of Ireland's past are other niche markets in which Lynchpin has established a presence.

The partners have built relationships with travel agents in America who attract groups of clients. A group of ten golfing surgeons from Chicago is typical of their core market. Other customers discover Lynchpin for themselves on the internet or through word-of-mouth recommendations.

David and Lowell have developed the business using a "golden thread" of people – suppliers, agents and clients, past and present. Their suppliers include organisations from other sectors of the travel and tourism industry such as hotels, coach companies, specialist guides and visitor attractions. Their approach has been to use a restricted number of suppliers (about 40) with whose owners and managers they have developed personal working relationships. This has helped them to develop Lynchpin's quality and reputation for personal service.

Galvin's Coaches of Limerick is a transport provider that supplies coaches for Lynchpin. By bringing Galvin's repeat business, Lowell, who deals with suppliers, has become able to request named drivers whom he knows will provide Lynchpin's clients with high quality customer service. Accommodation used by Lynchpin includes the three-star Gleann Fia guest house in Killarney, as well as a range of hotels throughout the country. Building a personal rapport with owners and managers has allowed David, who escorts tour groups, to successfully make special arrangements for clients on the spot, e.g. a request for a ground floor room not previously notified. It has also meant that customers see that David is known to the hotel's owners, helping them to feel secure and in safe hands. Such points have been included in recommendations that have led new customers to approach Lynchpin and book tours.

Lowell and David have found that they can compete in the market place by providing one-off quality products, at prices that are comparable to those of larger tour operators. To out-compete major companies, who benefit from economies of scale, on price would not be realistic. However Lynchpin has been able to grow by offering flexible, customer-centred packages that use good quality accommodation and sympathetic, knowledgeable guides. In short, sufficient customers, largely American customers, choose Lynchpin not because they are cheaper than their larger competitors, but because the company offers a high quality, more customised product.

Size and structure

Lynchpin is a partnership of two. David and Lowell own and run the business themselves. It is the smallness of the enterprise that allows them the flexibility to deal with each customer individually and to tailor tours to match specific needs. A small car may be nippy and turn quickly while a large truck may need more time and space to change direction. In the same way, a small tour business can quickly adapt to the particular demands of a client whereas a larger one may have more standardised products, which are less easy to adapt just to satisfy one customer or one small group of customers.

Lowell and David are equal partners. Each has his clearly defined role in the business (see Figure 4.3). Lowell is based in Lynchpin's office in Portrush. He deals with bookings, in both directions – from customers and dealing with the suppliers of package elements, such as accommodation and transport. Lowell discusses the planning of their tour with the client, usually over the telephone or by e-mail and develops the itinerary accordingly. He takes the customer's booking and negotiates accommodation, transport and attractions visits with suppliers. To maintain the quality of the product, Lowell seeks to ensure, for example, that hotel rooms (double or twin, ground floor or not, shower or bath) match what he now knows about the group and that his preferred driver will be at the wheel of the coach.

Price is important and is an issue that Lowell must keep under constant review. Clearly he needs to arrange to pay suppliers an amount that means

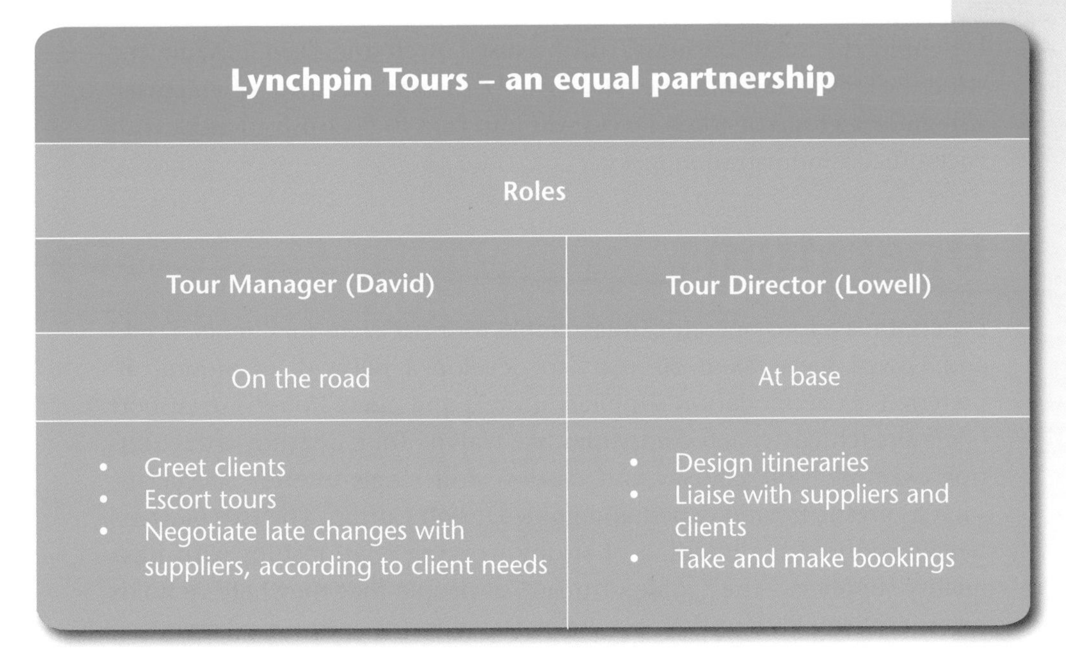

Lynchpin Tours – an equal partnership	
Roles	
Tour Manager (David)	Tour Director (Lowell)
On the road	At base
• Greet clients • Escort tours • Negotiate late changes with suppliers, according to client needs	• Design itineraries • Liaise with suppliers and clients • Take and make bookings

Figure 4.3 – The structure of Lynchpin Tours

Lynchpin will make a profit after charging customers a price they will see as reasonable and be happy to pay. This demands skill, not least because most of Lynchpin's customers pay in US dollars, the business is based in the sterling area (Northern Ireland) and suppliers are largely based in the Irish Republic where the currency is the Euro. Since exchange rates change daily, Lowell finds that he begins each morning by catching up with the current rates.

David does a lot of travelling in his role for Lynchpin. He escorts tours, often travelling by car independently of the group coach. In that way he can arrive at an attraction or the hotel ahead of the party. He smooths the way for their arrival, sorting out snags that may have arisen, for example with hotel room arrangements. When the party arrives they are met and can proceed seamlessly with their attraction visit or go directly to their rooms. Acting in this way, David is ensuring the quality of the customers' tour experience. Keen to maintain good relations with good suppliers, David always offers either to pay for his accommodation or suggests that he will stay elsewhere – perhaps in a bed and breakfast in the local town. He finds that this does not happen and suppliers accommodate him as the tour representative free of charge. He always accepts, provided the hotel will allow him to pay for his meal.

Lynchpin is a small business, run by just Lowell and David. While the structure is clear, it cannot be fully rigid. Occasions may arise when Lowell will guide a group or when David will join him in Portrush to assist with back-office administration tasks.

Operations

Lynchpin is a tour operator. To assemble tour packages for clients, David and Lowell have taken 10 years to develop a network of around 40 preferred accommodation suppliers (hotels and guest houses), transport operators (chiefly coach companies like Galvin Tours), visitor attractions (for example, golf courses and castles) and single-interest specialists, such as mystic Ireland expert and guide Dr Bob Curran. The two partners have prioritised the building of strong working relationships with high quality suppliers – the "golden thread" of people that they believe holds together the quality of their products. David is out on the road escorting tours. He builds the links with suppliers that Lowell uses to design special interest tours of Ireland that he customises for each client. Lowell's initial contacts with customers are telephone calls or messages and e-mails. Direct contact comes from interested potential customers who have been attracted to Lynchpin's website on the internet www.lynchpintours.com, or through word-of-mouth recommendation. On other occasions, one of Lynchpin's American agents will telephone or e-mail Lowell to discuss possible arrangements for groups of clients who have come to them to help arrange a tour of Ireland.

Sample itineraries have been made available on the website. Lowell can use these and clients' immediate thoughts to begin to design a customised itinerary proposal. He sets out to try and discover as much as he can about what customers want from their tour of Ireland and understand their needs, for example types of accommodation, dietary requirements, special interests, etc. Based on his findings Lowell drafts a potential outline itinerary and then begins to telephone relevant suppliers from Lynchpin's preferred suppliers' list. Establishing availability and negotiating price he can begin to firm up his proposal, which he then discusses with the client. Following any adjustments made as a result of that consultation, Lowell has a priced itinerary to present to the customer, at a price he hopes they will find attractive. That being the case, he is able to take their booking and deposit, which is usually paid by credit card.

Many of Lynchpin's customers are from North America. Americans not only find credit cards a convenient way to pay Lynchpin, but many also like to use them to gain more Air Miles or similar reward points – perhaps to put towards their next trip "over the pond".

A growing line of business for Lynchpin has been tours for small groups of customers who arrive in an Irish port such as Belfast or Dublin on board a cruise ship. Cruise lines provide their own excursions of course, but these are often charged as optional extras and involve coach loads of people at a time. Lynchpin offer smaller-scale customised, personally guided tours to cruise passengers. Prices are similar to those charged by cruise operators. David meets such groups at the port. He may personally drive a small party in an executive mini-coach. Alternatively he will introduce them to the driver that Lowell has specifically requested from their preferred coach supplier and drive ahead by car to the first attraction, for example from Belfast port to the Giant's Causeway. Arriving first he can make sure the party are expected, are fully ticketed and can progress smoothly on with their visit as he greets them on their arrival. He does the same thing at each hotel. During the visit David talks informally with customers to elicit from them any personal wishes they may hope to fulfil while they are in the area and to see what he can do to help.

For example, conversations with a party of golfers in the Shannon area led David to discover that one was an aeroplane enthusiast. He proposed and arranged a spontaneous side-trip to the Foynes Flying Boat Museum (see Figure 4.4). This "going the extra mile" benefits Lynchpin because it helps them build a reputation for flexibility and personal service, leading to repeat business and recommendation to potential future clients. Websites such as Trip Advisor attract travellers' comments that can play an important part in generating future trade. Lynchpin's partners particularly value word-of-mouth recommendations. Their view is that potential customers place more weight on recommendations from friends and colleagues who they know than those that are made by anonymous website contributors.

***Figure 4.4** – Foynes Flying Boat Museum, County Limerick*

People management

The "golden thread" of people is central to Lynchpin's way of doing business. It applies to staffing and to the management of human resources as well as in the sphere of customer service.

The two partners themselves, Lowell and David, are Lynchpin's permanent staff. Since they are equal partners neither is in charge of the other and so neither manages the other. However, they do both need to manage their relationship with each other. They are old friends. Arguably this helps, as does the fact that they have defined roles within Lynchpin. Each supports the other in their particular aspect of the operation and they have a shared vision for their business. They both see it as remaining quite small, specialising in tours of Ireland and providing a customised service to small groups who accept the need to pay for personalised attention. Because David's role takes him out on the road while Lowell is more office-based they do not spend every working day together either.

Lynchpin's other human resources, apart from the two partners, are the people who supply services to them. They maintain a database of, altogether, 40 preferred suppliers of accommodation, transport, guiding services and attraction visits. For each of these they have a list of three back-up suppliers, to use in the event that the preferred supplier cannot deliver – perhaps in the case of a sudden, short-notice booking or cancellation by an initial supplier. The success of tours depends on negotiating arrangements that are tailor-made for customers. So, the maintenance of good relationships with suppliers is vital. Lynchpin's policy of paying providers immediately, rather than settling invoices 60-90 days later, which is common practice in the Irish Republic where 90% of Lynchpin's suppliers are based, is appreciated by suppliers and helps "oil the wheels" of this business relationship.

The other aim of Lynchpin's human resources management is to keep product quality high. For example, by only using the same five coach drivers they know and trust to do a good job for them, Lynchpin helps to ensure that customers are happy and more likely to recommend them to others later. This means that Lowell has to be in a position to insist that a coach supplier provides Lynchpin with the driver he wants. One of the results of maintaining good supplier relationships is that this does place him in a position to ask for, and nearly always be offered, his named driver.

Lynchpin's customer service policy is "to go the extra mile on all occasions". Itineraries are put together through direct consultation with customers. David escorts tours to keep up the personal link with clients. Examples of little extras that can make real differences are Lynchpin's willingness to make telephone calls to help trace North American clients' living Irish relatives prior to their visit, making mobile phone arrangements for customers so they do not find that their cell phone will not work when they arrive in Ireland and tracking back through tours to trace lost property inadvertently left behind in accommodation or at visitor attractions.

Finance/funding

Lynchpin is privately financed. That is to say the partners themselves provided the capital needed to set up the business. However, it is not a capital-intensive business, i.e. it does not require large sums of money in the form of bank loans to keep it operating on a profitable basis. Many costs are generated and then covered by each tour and its pricing. On-going overheads are relatively minimal, mostly related to maintaining and running the office in Portrush. With no permanent staff other than the partners, there is no wages bill.

Accounts for each financial year are audited by April. The business is profitable (total income is greater than total expenditure) and solvent, i.e. it has sufficient funds to carry on setting up tours since the necessary re-funding is covered by the income received from clients on organised tours.

***Figure 4.5** – Irish heritage features heavily in Lynchpin's tours* (courtesy of Tourism Ireland)

Marketing

The main selling points for Lynchpin are its smallness, its personalised approach and its emphasis on quality; these are linked. Because of its size (the two partners being the only permanent staff), Lynchpin is able to adapt tours to suit the personal needs of clients. By having one of the partners escort tours, it is well placed to assure the quality of the customer experience.

Lynchpin promotes itself as the only Northern Ireland-based tour operator to have substantial experience of the whole of Ireland – North and South. Partners David and Lowell believe that this has given them a competitive edge over potential rivals. Marketing Lynchpin's products takes place, says Lowell, "every time you talk to someone". So, he follows up e-mail enquiries with personal telephone calls (many of which are transatlantic) to make human contact with potential customers, assess their needs

***Figure 4.6** – Lynchpin's website* **www.lynchpintours.com**

and move the process forward towards making a sale. In designing and proposing possible itineraries, Lowell tries to show clients a creative approach to differentiate Lynchpin from any other operator they may be considering using.

"Channels of distribution" are the routes by which Lynchpin makes its products available to customers. Lynchpin makes limited use of web marketing and Comcast videos, but the partners see people as the most important means of spreading the word about their products and services. Satisfied customers are valued for their role in raising awareness within the target market segment of adult, special interest groups. Such potential customers often visit the Lynchpin website next. In this way the internet is also an important marketing tool. However, it has its limits. Among the target market, the internet is often viewed with a degree of scepticism by potential customers. While they may well view the website as a valuable source of information, they can be mistrustful of open access sites such as Trip Adviser and prefer the confirmation of recommendation from an existing customer when possible. Consequently, comments from past guests are posted on the Lynchpin website.

The blog, however, is a growing e-marketing avenue for Lynchpin. Lowell uses blogs to further raise Lynchpin's e-profile. In addition, Lynchpin's website includes a hyperlink facility that allows browsers to sign up for Lynchpin's newsletter and e-mail updates. Another allows the user to request a telephone callback from Tour Director Lowell, thus combining e-marketing and personal contact.

Figure 4.7 shows the Lynchpin logo. The actual name "Lynchpin" implies marketing messages of:

- Irish heritage – a lynchpin is an element of traditional costume;
- Holding together (the tour package) – since that is what traditional lynchpin does;
- Being the key element – on which success depends.

***Figure 4.7** – Lynchpin's logo*

Lynchpin's emphasis on producing personalised tours for each client is itself a marketing strategy. Aware of their target market, the partners promote their business, via the website, as concentrating on individual needs, "while most tour operators concentrate on filling buses and meeting schedules".

Future

David and Lowell look to the future with optimism. They have no ambition for Lynchpin to grow greatly, nor any intention that it should become a major tour operator. Their business plan is for it to remain a small, specialist tour company, operating at the premium end of the market, continuing to provide personalised tours of Ireland for customers who are prepared to pay a premium price for a quality product.

While they expect that the USA will continue to provide the bulk of their customer base, they are alive to expansion opportunities offered by e-marketing. Lowell's blog contributions, for example, have led to enquiries from potential new markets including South Africa.

Lynchpin's short-term future strategy involves developing the use of primary market research, analysing data gleaned from "good" past clients (fully satisfied customers who fit the profile of their intended market) to help produce value for money tours that will straightaway appeal to like-minded people. The partners' expectation is that this will not only generate more immediate business, but also lead to a snowball effect, with future recommendations very likely.

Issues to consider

1. Lynchpin deals daily in three currencies (Sterling, U.S. Dollars and Euros). Exchange rates are beyond Lynchpin's control. Relative rates change constantly and can be highly volatile. When the Dollar value of the Euro is high, turnover suffers, though the reverse is also periodically true. Exchange rate fluctuation represents a risk to the business.

CONSIDER: How and why Lynchpin's future may depend on currency fluctuations.

2. The personalised service the partners can offer because of the business's small-scale is in the end self-limiting to future growth. They rely on their reputation built through word-of-mouth to generate repeat business. Rapid growth would make it hard to maintain high quality personal service.

CONSIDER: Whether small-scale personal service organisations like Lynchpin have an in-built weakness when it comes to expansion.

3. The "golden thread" of supplier, agent and customer contacts is strong and valuable. However, it is a thread - it could snap or be cut. This might happen if, for instance, a key supplier suddenly went out of business or if American customers were to lose confidence in transatlantic travel.

CONSIDER: The actions Lynchpin's partners would need to take in the case of either of the above two eventualities.

4. Lynchpin is based in Northern Ireland but operates mostly in the Republic. The partners have found it more to difficult to build the

kind of links with suppliers in the North that they have come to rely upon with accommodation providers in the South.

CONSIDER: To what extent future competitive weakness may stem from reliance on southern business for a north of Ireland enterprise like Lynchpin.

5. As the only Northern Ireland based tour operator to provide a broad portfolio of personalised, special interest tours in the Republic, Lynchpin has been pioneering. It took them a decade to establish their all-Ireland quality supplier network.

CONSIDER: How vulnerable Lynchpin is to 'copycat' competition.

6. Clients expect the facility to book Lynchpin's tours directly online. Competition means that Lynchpin must offer it via their website. However, customers can make mistakes and quite often do. This is an extra source of cost.

CONSIDER: How extra costs arise from customer self-booking online.

7. The partners feel that they could provide more transparency in pricing their tours, with itemised costs for instance, so that customers could see that they really are being offered a square deal. Lynchpin have found that their largely American clientelle is generally happy to pay a premium, confident of a professional service, for having the strain and responsibility of tour planning taken from their shoulders.

CONSIDER: The extent to which price is not always the prime consideration for a customer making a purchasing decision.

Discussion questions

(differentiated by level)

1. Attempt a SWOT analysis of Lynchpin Tours (Level3/GCE AS).

2. What's in a name? Analyse the marketing advantages of a travel and tourism brand name other than Lynchpin (Level 3/GCE A2).

3. What strengths and weaknesses do Lynchpin's size and structure give the business? (Level 3/GCE A2).

4. Comment on the significance of the internet to Lynchpin's operations (Level 3/GCE AS).

5. To what extent does the long-term future of the business lie in the partners' own hands? (GCE A2/Foundation Degree).

6. Recommend a course of action to Lynchpin's partners that should ensure the continued future success of the business. You may find it useful to research approaches taken by other successful, small-scale tour businesses (Foundation Degree).

Ocean Village

– a cruise operator

Introduction

Ocean Village operates two cruise ships – Ocean Village and Ocean Village Two. It markets fly-cruise holidays in the Caribbean during the northern hemisphere winter and offers Mediterranean cruises in the summer.

Ocean Village's idea is to offer a different style of cruising holiday that appeals to customers who have not been on this type of holiday before and who would not otherwise think of doing so. Ocean Village cruises are 'new cruises'. They are targeted at a younger clientele; traditionally cruises have appealed to mature and senior adult age groups. More than half of Ocean Village's passengers are first-time cruisers. The average age of Ocean Village passengers, just 43 in the summer season, is over ten years younger than the cruising market's norm.

New cruises, such as those marketed by Ocean Village (see Figure 5.1), place more emphasis on physical activities, for example an onboard gym and mountain biking ashore, plus frequent destination visits (typically six per week's cruise). The formal rituals of life on board a conventional cruise ship, such as dressing for dinner, have been dropped.

History and development

Ocean Village is a relatively new company that began operating cruise holidays in 2003. Since then, it has been developing a new style of product – the 'new cruise'. This is a more informal, more active product aimed at a younger target market. Ocean Village has been successful in developing this concept and has won various awards including:

- Best Mainstream Cruise Line – 2005 British Travel Awards;
- Best Mediterranean Cruise Operator and Best Budget Cruise Operator – Selling Cruises Awards 2005;
- Best Specialist Cruise Line – Travel Globe Awards 2006;
- Best Cruise Line – Observer and Guardian Newspaper Travel Awards 2006;
- Best Cruise and Ferry Website – Travelmole Awards 2007.

***Figure 5.1** – Ocean Village markets a new type of cruising*

In 2007, Ocean Village expanded its operations by introducing its second ship, Ocean Village Two. This began cruising the western Mediterranean that summer, sailing out of Palma, Mallorca from May to October. Meanwhile, the original Ocean Village ship changed its base port to Heraklion in Crete so that the company could introduce island-hopping cruises in the eastern Mediterranean.

Ocean Village's development has not been the result of attracting customers away from existing, conventional cruise operators – 60% of Ocean Village's customers are actually first-time cruisers. The company has been instrumental in, and has benefited from, a new buoyancy in the whole cruising market. The number of British tourists taking cruise holidays doubled in the ten years to 2006 to reach a total of 1.3m. The Passenger Shipping Association predicted a further 8% growth in 2007 and 15% in 2008.

In the 'golden age' of passenger ships, in the early and mid-twentieth century, Southampton was the starting point for many transatlantic cruise ships and in the 1950s had 8 passenger terminals. Yet in 2007 the gross tonnage of passenger ships in the port of Southampton on the date Ocean Village Two's launch (April 24) was almost double the port's 1950s maximum. Two of the world's largest passenger ships were in port on the launch day (Queen Mary 2 and Liberty of the Seas), as was P&O's Oriana. The four ships had a combined passenger-handling capacity of 20,440 passengers, based on one set of passengers leaving and another joining the ships that day. This indicates that cruising holidays are a major travel and tourism product for the early twenty-first century, which the Ocean Village brand is tapping with its new-style of casual cruises.

Structure

Ocean Village is owned by Carnival, which is the world's largest cruise company. Carnival plc's other well-known cruising brands include P&O Cruises, Cunard, Swan Hellenic and Princess Cruises. Carnival plc is the UK arm of the transnational Carnival Corporation, whose global headquarters are in Miami, Florida.

Business operations such as sales and staff recruitment are organised by Carnival plc across the P&O Cruises, Cunard, Princess Cruises and Ocean Village Holidays brands. This is partly because of the company's past history – P&O Princess Cruises was an independent public limited company (plc) until it merged with Carnival in 2003.

Operations

Ocean Village cruises are in the Mediterranean during the summer months (May to October) and in the Caribbean during the European winter. At the change of season, longer cruises are offered. Examples are from Crete to Southampton in October, from Southampton across the Atlantic to Jamaica in November and from Jamaica to Crete in April.

The core products are fly-cruises starting from a choice of UK airports. Cruises are 7 or 14 nights long and can be added to a week's hotel stay in Barbados, Majorca or Crete to put together a two week 'stay and cruise' package holiday.

Both Ocean Village ships are equipped and fitted out in the style of the Ocean Village brand image with the intention of appealing to a younger adult market than may always be the case with some of Carnival's other cruising brands. Ocean Village's ships' facilities include gym, spa, pool, Jacuzzi, health and beauty salon, mountain bikes for exploring ashore, cinema, casino, childcare, a teenage zone and a choice of restaurants and bars. A particular selling point for Ocean Village is the high number of cabins with private outside balconies – on Ocean Village Two there are nearly 200 of these, and more than 600 of the 800-plus cabins are on the outside of the vessel.

Customer service

Since most of Ocean Village's customers have not previously been on a cruising holiday, there is a more than usual need for customer information and support in advance of holidays taking place. This is added to by the fact that for many of the 40% who have cruised before, their past cruising experiences were not of the rather different, less formal style that Ocean Village has been developing.

Fundamental questions that need to be addressed in order to serve cruise customers well include:

- What should I pack?
- Do I need cash on board?
- How will I get ashore?
- Will mobile 'phones work on board?
- Are towels provided on the ships?
- What facilities are provided for families?

Such basic questions may matter a great deal to the first-time booker, but can also be time consuming for staff to answer individually. To attract trade from an essentially new customer base, Ocean Village has developed a strong information and marketing package (see the Marketing section on page 54). Frequently asked questions (FAQs) such as those listed above are addressed there. Figure 5.2 is a summary of answers to a range of Ocean Village customer information requests.

Customer question	Summary Ocean Village response
What should I pack?	Casual wear. The only place to dress more formally is in The Bistro (one of the onboard restaurants). On 'Stay and Cruise' holidays, smart casual clothes/ long trousers for dinner may be required by some hotels.
Do I need cash on board?	There is a 'cash-free' system on board. Customers sign for what they spend and then settle up at the end.
How will I get ashore?	Usually passengers can come and go as they please via the ship's gangway. In some ports the ship anchors at sea and boats transfer passengers to the port.
Do I need a passport or visa?	A full passport valid for 6 months after return from holiday is required. Children under 16 need travel documents too. Normally full British Citizen passport-holders do not need visas.
What facilities are provided for families?	Families are invited to an informal meeting at the start of the holiday where the ship's Youth Team explain child and teenage facilities on board, what activities are planned each day and what restrictions there are that affect children.
Will mobile 'phones work on board?	No (2007), although this may change.

Figure 5.2 *– Ocean Village customer service – some FAQs*

Dealing with access and mobility issues, which some of its customers may experience, is part of Ocean Village's service to its customers. The two Ocean Village ships are accessible to wheelchair and mobility scooter users. There are lifts and wheelchair/scooter access to most public areas on board, as well as to cabins specially adapted for wheelchair users. Such adaptations include wide doorways and bathrooms featuring wheel-in showers.

Mobility is a particularly significant customer service issue for Ocean Village crews helping cruise passengers to go ashore. Means for wheelchair users to get ashore are not always available at all ports of call. Ocean Village crews use a short low-level gangway, called the ship's brow, to give wheelchair users access to the shore when they can. Each of the two ships also carries a wheelchair 'stair climbing' machine to use when the ship's brow cannot be used.

At ports where an Ocean Village ship cannot dock at the quayside, passengers are taken ashore by launch boat. Crew members help wheelchair users who are able to bear their own weight in and out of the launches. However, health and safety regulations mean that the crew are not allowed to physically lift passengers into launches. Ocean Village transfer wheelchairs to the quay and staff can assist dismantling and assembling wheelchairs on request. Nonetheless, customers and/or travelling companions are responsible for doing so safely.

Funding Ocean Village Two

Ocean Village's ships were not purpose-built for the brand but were refurbished to the necessary specifications from existing cruise ships. Ocean Village Two was previously called the AidaBlu when it was run by the German cruise operator Aida. Both Ocean Village and Aida are owned by Carnival, so a brand-to-brand transfer was relatively easy and funding the building or purchase of a wholly new ship was not necessary. Indeed the cost was further reduced because the AidaBlu had already been fitted out for casual-style 'new cruises' for Aida customers.

Marketing

An Ocean Village cruise is marketed as a new product – 'The cruise for people who don't do cruises'. The target market is adults in the 30-50 age bracket who enjoy exploring new places and trying new activities. Ocean Village shore trips are themselves sub-branded 'Action Ashore', to help create an image that will appeal to the chosen market segment. Informality is the keynote of Ocean Village promotions. The restrictions found on conventional cruises, such as set meal times and strict dress codes, do not apply to Ocean Village cruises, so the 'wear what you want and eat when the mood takes you' message is emphasised at all times.

Ocean Village has adopted innovative approaches to promoting its brand. It is specifically targeting customers who do not normally buy its core product – a cruise holiday – and so, to grab their attention, it needs to stand out from the crowd. To back up the promotion of its 'for people who don't do cruises' strap line in media advertisements, Ocean Village accompanies direct home mailing of its brochure with a high production value promotional DVD. People seen in the DVD are firmly within the target age group and activities and relaxing spa facilities are strongly featured with an upbeat soundtrack.

Some 60% of Ocean Village customers have indeed been 'people who don't do cruises', in that their Ocean Village holiday was the first cruise

Figure 5.3 – The Ocean Village website

they had taken. Ocean Village's primary competition is not with cruise operators but with the operators of beach holidays. Market research has found that Ocean Village attracts customers who have previously patronised operators of traditional beach and all-inclusive holidays.

The Ocean Village website www.oceanvillageholidays.co.uk has also broken new ground, by featuring an online virtual tour as early as 2003. In 2007 the Ocean Village website won the Travelmole award for Best Cruise and Ferry Website.

Future

Ocean Village intends to respond to social and market trends to continue attracting first-time cruising customers. One such trend is the growing proportion of the market made up of single parent families. Between summer 2005 and summer 2006, the company noted a 26% increase in single parents travelling with two children. It was because of this that Ocean Village Two was purposely fitted with 100 specially configured 3-berth cabins. These cabins are furnished with a pair of standard twin beds and a further fold-away bed.

Ocean Village aims to have increasing numbers of single parent families as customers. This is because while one-parent families now account for about 25% of the family market, that proportion is expected to continue to grow until at least 2020. In addition, increasingly more two-parent families holiday separately, with one parent taking the children on holiday while the other remains working.

Issues to consider

1. 60% of Ocean Village customers are people who haven't been on a cruise before. Marketing is pitched at just this group. Travel and tourism organisations usually rely to some extent on the repeat business of established and returning customers.

CONSIDER: How Ocean Village can keep attracting new customers while retaining its existing clientele.

2. Ocean Village's target market is 30-50 year olds. However, relatively youthful, active adults do age! Keeping forever young can be more of an aspiration that a reality.

CONSIDER: Whether Ocean Village should aim to keep a relatively youthful image.

3. Ocean Village insists that each wheelchair-using customer is accompanied by a fit and able-bodied travelling companion – one able-bodied companion per wheelchair user. None of Ocean Village's hotels on shore offer specific disabled access or facilities and are not suitable for wheelchair users.

CONSIDER: The extent to which these restrictions are fair and reasonable for Ocean Village and its customers.

4. Ocean Village's Caribbean ports of call are destinations in the less developed world. There is rising awareness among Ocean Village's target market of the desirability of responsible tourism practice.

CONSIDER: (a) The likely impacts of large cruise vessels such as the Ocean Village ship on a Caribbean port and island; (b) How Ocean Village can promote responsible tourism practices among its passengers.

5. The UK cruising market shows seasonal tourist flow patterns with summer Mediterranean and winter Caribbean cruises.

CONSIDER: The reasons for these patterns and how Ocean Village has adapted to them.

Discussion questions

(differentiated by level)

1. The average age of Ocean Village passengers (43, in the summer season) is over ten years younger than the cruising market's norm. Explain how Ocean Village uses product and promotion to target adults aged 30-50 (Level 3/GCE A2).

2. Ocean Village is a brand owned by the global cruise company Carnival, whose other brand divisions include P&O Cruises, Cunard and Princess Cruises. Analyse the distinctiveness of these Carnival brands (Level 3/GCE A2).

3. Recommend and justify the policy you think a small Caribbean island government should adopt towards cruise ships calling (GCE A2/Foundation Degree).

4. 'Large cruise ships are really just all-inclusive hotels that move. Their impacts are all the more unsustainable as a result.' Discuss this statement (Foundation Degree).

Expedia

– an online travel company

Introduction

Expedia is an online travel company, whose website www.expedia.co.uk, is the online booking website provided for its British customers by the US-based, international corporation Expedia. Customers access Expedia's website to research and book travel, accommodation and other tourism products and services.

***Figure 6.1** – Expedia's UK website*

History and development

Founded in 1995 as part of the Microsoft Corporation, Expedia launched its US website in 1996. Expedia's UK website went online in 1998 as the company began its international expansion into Europe as well as Canada. As internet use expanded after the millennium, the company developed rapidly in the UK from a small customer base of 'in-the-know' independent travellers and early internet users to a much more mainstream business with a wide appeal to the general travelling public.

In 2002-3 Expedia's ownership changed. The business was under the umbrella of the American InterActive Corp (IAC) organisation until 2005 when IAC and Expedia Inc separated into two distinct enterprises.

However, as the first decade of the 21st century wore on, the earlier rapid expansion in the company's website hit rate began to slow. Television and mass media advertising was used to raise awareness among the growing numbers of customers able to make use of their home computers to arrange their own trips by booking flights, transfers, accommodation and extra services via a single website – the internet equivalent of the 'one-stop shop'. The growing availability of high-speed broadband internet connections and wireless networks in homes further assisted the continued early 21st century development of online travel companies such as Expedia. Much quicker web surfing and site navigation made them considerably more user-friendly and price competitive in comparison to conventional travel agent shops and, perhaps more particularly, telephone-based direct-sell tour operators. Figure 6.2 summarises the products and services available via Expedia's UK home page.

Structure

Expedia Inc is the world's largest online travel company. As well as selling travel and tourism products and services to retail customers, Expedia also provides wholesale travel products for offline travel agents to sell on to consumers. Expedia Inc's brands in the UK include:

1. Expedia.co.uk – online travel booking;

2. Hotels.co.uk – hotel information and booking;

Products	Services
• Air flights • Car hire • Eurostar rail travel • Airport transfers	• Online booking • Online information such as flight timetables
• Hotel accommodation • Ski and snowboard rental • Sightseeing tours • Admission to shows and events, including sporting events • Theme park admission	• Online tourism guides to destinations • Online maps of destinations
• Package holidays • Tailor-made holidays • Insurance policies • Corporate travel (including accommodation)	• Online customer support • E-mail alerts of special offers • Personalised online accounts

Figure 6.2– *Products and services on Expedia's UK website*

3. Expedia Corporate Travel – business travel services;
4. Trip Advisor – a hotel and destination reviews website with links to Expedia and other travel websites for making travel reservations.

Expedia companies currently operate online travel websites in Australia, Canada, Denmark, France, Germany, Italy, Japan, the Netherlands, Norway, Spain, Sweden, the United Kingdom and China.

North American brands not currently available in the UK include Hotwire and Classic Vacations, while Expedia Europe, based in France, has Anyway.com (a discount air travel provider) and Voyages-SNCF.fr, an online rail travel website operated in partnership with France's state-owned railway.

Operations

Expedia operates in both the wholesale and retail travel and tourism markets. In the wholesale market, the organisation makes its products available to retail travel agents, while in the retail market it sells travel, accommodation and support services directly to consumers.

Expedia operates online, but is neither simply a travel agent nor simply a tour operator. It is both, which is why it, and similar organisations such as Travelocity, lastminute.com and Opodo, are classified as online travel companies or online bookers. They transcend the travel agent and tour operator stages of the traditional chain of distribution for travel products (see Figure 6.3). Expedia acts as a travel agent when it sells products provided by its partner suppliers to its customers (whether in the wholesale or in the retail market). Principals, such as airlines, tour operators and hotel accommodation providers, agree terms with Expedia for it to sell their products online, often at discounted prices.

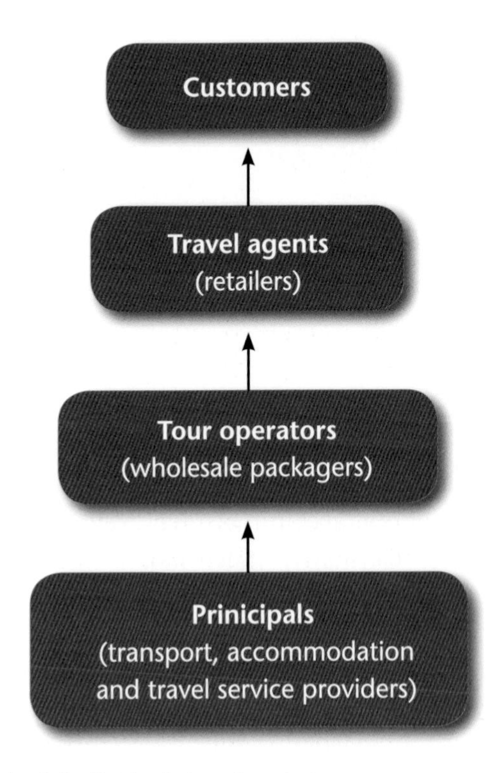

***Figure 6.3** – The chain of distribution in travel products*

Expedia behaves as a tour operator when it combines the products of principals into the pre-packaged holidays that it then sells on its website. Many of Expedia's customers self-package their own holidays, a concept known as 'dynamic packaging'. They browse the website for trip components such as flights, hotels and car hire, often not buying them as separate items but as package deals at discounted prices. In this way Expedia's website is operating as a tour operating facility. When Expedia sells its customers tour operator products via its UK website, the customers agree the legal terms and conditions of their bookings with Apollo Travel, a subsidiary of the UK travel agent Co-op Travel, which is based in Stoke-on-Trent.

Online travel companies such as Expedia are blurring the traditional travel and tourism industry distinction between travel agents and tour operators. They represent a form of vertical integration that is different from that exemplified by major players like Thomson/TUI (see Case Study 15), which have become vertically-integrated via the acquisition of once separate travel agent, tour operator, transport principal and accommodation provider businesses.

Customer service

The default customer experience of Expedia is person-free. Travel and tourism is sometimes described as a 'people industry', largely because of the number of inter-personal exchanges involved in providing travel products and services to customers. Online travel companies are breaking this mould by providing an anonymous, 'virtual' buying experience for customers.

Nevertheless, it is vital for any travel and tourism organisation's profitability that repeat customer business is attracted. The quality of customer service is a major factor in doing this. So, the challenge for an online travel company such as Expedia is to provide a website that delivers accurate, reliable and supportive customer service.

Ease of comprehension and use are important attributes of the Expedia homepage (see Figure 6.1). The basic product and service navigation routes are straightforwardly listed along a button bar at the top of the page. Returning registered users are personally greeted by name. This feel-good device is helpful in attracting existing customers to book again and enticing the customer who has previously only browsed the site to make a purchase. Sale closure is, from the travel and tourism organisation's point of view, a vital part of customer service – the ultimate goal of a successful staff-customer interchange. The website provides a rapid and direct 'book now' route for key flight and hotel products straight from the home page as well as information about promotions and links to allow the exploration of travel options on other pages of the site.

Other services provided via Expedia's website include access to free tourist guide information about destinations and their attractions, with options to access and print online maps and driving directions. Other services include providing access to insurance cover and the setting up of a personal account online so that customers can review the progress of arrangements they are making. Like many commercial organisations, Expedia offers a changing list of special deals that can be communicated to customers by e-mail. A growing interactive section deals with opportunities to share and review travel experiences with other customers. Such services help engender a feeling of belonging on the part of browsing customers who, by being kept on-site, are more likely to make purchase decisions before leaving than if they had had to exit the site to do background research and then make the additional decision to return to buy. Other online travel company websites are easily accessible and present competing intervening opportunities to the customer (threats to Expedia), so retaining customers within the Expedia web environment is important in closing down this threat.

Finance

Financially, Expedia Inc is a major transnational organisation. The total business generates more than US $17 billion of travel bookings per year. In the third quarter of 2007 alone, gross profit was approximately $300 million. This was an increase of some 27% compared with the equivalent period in 2006. Expedia attributed the rise to a combination of greater turnover and bigger operating profit margins. The latter were largely due to efficiency savings in operating costs. Expedia Inc's international businesses, those beyond the USA and including Expedia UK, amounted to roughly one-third of the corporation's worldwide bookings. This compared to 27% in the prior year period, so it is perhaps not surprising that one of Expedia's future intentions is to further increase its global presence in new international markets.

Marketing

Two key targets for Expedia's marketing efforts are:

- Individual business and leisure consumers;
- Other travel and tourism organisations.

Expedia's initial tourist customers were largely experienced, independent travellers. In competing with conventional providers to make in-roads into the wider market, Expedia has needed to win the confidence of customers who have traditionally been happy to buy package holidays from travel agents and direct-sell tour operators. Expedia has been assisted by the general market trend of package holiday decline and independent travel growth, but has deployed marketing tools to build consumer confidence among those tourists who feel less secure about making their own travel arrangements or booking online without personal contact.

Identity theft and financial protection in the event of an air travel trip going wrong perhaps leaving the customer stranded abroad are two of the top concerns among the less confident section of the market into which Expedia has been making in-roads. With regard to the former, Expedia publishes a privacy pledge on its website, promising to 'ensure the security and confidentiality of personally identifiable information (PII)'. PII is information that can be linked to a specific person, for example name, address, telephone number and e-mail address.

Air travel holidays are protected under the Air Travel Organisers' Licensing (ATOL) scheme. Regulated by the Civil Aviation Authority (CAA), this is a customer protection scheme safeguarding tourists in the event of a tour operator ceasing to trade, including when customers are on holiday overseas. Trips booked online through Expedia generate vouchers and confirmation for transfers, accommodation, attractions and excursions which customers print for themselves. Some customers demand the reassurance that all will be well if the overseas provider will not accept these for any reason.

Expedia sells the products of other travel and tourism providers on its website, but does not provide an online booking service for all travel and tourism organisations, just those that it refers to as 'partner suppliers'. Partners enter into contractual agreements with Expedia which features their products on its website, provides an online booking service for them and, so, increases their trade volume and their turnover. To expand its own business, Expedia uses its website to promote the advantages of becoming a partner. Hotel providers, for example, are encouraged to become an Expedia Special Rate hotel, meaning one at which Expedia customers can buy accommodation at discounted prices. The Expedia listing is free for the hotel and its management can reasonably expect that rooms that might otherwise have been unoccupied will be sold.

Future

Expedia's vision for the next decade is to continue to develop innovative ways for its customers to 'plan, purchase and share their travel experiences'. The company plans to develop the website itself, introducing new tools and technical features as internet technology continues to develop. It wants to further build brand awareness in countries where it is established, such as the UK, while branching out into others where it is not. In 2007, for example, Expedia launched new online point of sale websites in Austria (www.expedia.at) and New Zealand (www.expedia.co.nz). Equally, Expedia hopes to widen the range of its travel products and services even further by developing co-operative relationships with additional partner suppliers, such as airlines, tourist attractions and hotel providers.

Issues to consider

1. Expedia intends to continue to grow as an online travel company.

CONSIDER: How continued expansion may be possible now that easy internet access is so widespread.

2. Expedia faces competition from other travel and tourism organisations.

CONSIDER: (a) the range of Expedia's online competitors in the UK market place; and (b) the degree of threat posed by organisations which are not online specialists.

3. Secure online booking arrangements and robust confidentiality arrangements are important in maintaining customer confidence in the internet as a means of buying travel and tourism products.

CONSIDER: What Expedia can do to persuade potential customers that its website is safe and secure.

4. Expedia has a wide product range, but is looking for ways to expand its portfolio.

CONSIDER: Possible expansion of the range of products and services available through the expedia.co.uk website.

5. The internet is becoming increasingly interactive.

CONSIDER: The opportunities that are likely to arise for Expedia as the internet becomes increasingly interactive.

Discussion questions

(differentiated by level)

1. How have recent technological and product developments affected the growth of online travel companies such as Expedia? (Level 3/ GCE A2).

2. To what extent has Expedia's development followed the model of the product life cycle? (Level 3/GCE A2).

3. Make a reasoned assessment of the future prospects for online travel companies such as Expedia (GCE A2/Foundation Degree).

bmi

– an airline

Introduction

bmi (formerly known as British Midland Airways) is a UK airline operating scheduled services. bmibaby is bmi's subsidiary brand, operating in the budget/low-cost/no frills flight market. Altogether British Midland operates 1,600 flights per week over a route network that links airports in the UK, Europe and long-haul destinations in India, Saudi Arabia, the USA and the Caribbean.

History and development

British Midland actually started as a flight training school for RAF pilots in 1938, just before the outbreak of World War 2. After the war ended, the company diversified and began running passenger and cargo air charter services under the name Derby Aviation. In the 1950s it stopped training RAF pilots altogether to concentrate full-time on air transport provision (passenger and freight).

During the 1960s the then Derby Airways was one of the first UK air charter businesses to begin to exploit the growing package holidays market. The company changed its name to British Midland Airways in 1964 and moved its base from Burnaston near Derby to the newly-opened East Midlands Airport in the following year. British Midland Airways merged with Invica Airways in 1969.

***Figure7.1** – A bmi transatlantic Airbus A330*

Expansion continued through the 1970s as the company began to operate some long-haul services as well as diversifying again into aircraft leasing. As British Midland Airways Leasing the company began to lease long and short-haul aircraft types to 25 other airlines around the world. In 1979 British Midland Airways carried over one million passengers in a year for the first time.

In 1982 the company established its headquarters at Castle Donington, near East Midlands Airport. By the middle of the decade its telephone reservations centre was handling 25,000 calls a week and passenger numbers had risen to 1.8 million per year. Having shortened its name to British Midland in 1986, the company introduced its first frequent flyer loyalty scheme, called Diamond Club, in 1987.

In an environment in which British Midland's main competitors were flag-carrier airlines, such as British Airways and Air France, its success depended upon having sufficient capital investment to develop innovative approaches that would attract custom. Scandinavian Airlines and Lufthansa, as non-UK flag-carriers, both invested in the company during the 1990s. By the end of the decade, British Midland was carrying 6.5 million passengers a year, and these two European principals each owned 20% of its business.

Innovations included becoming the first airline to offer a vegetarian meal option to passengers on UK services (1992) and the first European carrier to offer a separate business class cabin. Significantly, British Midland became the first airline to offer an online booking service with payment as early as 1995.

British Midland joined the Star Alliance on 1 July 2000. Star Alliance is a grouping of independent airlines from around the world which co-operate with each other to provide a global network of flights that is considerably greater than each individual member could operate by itself. Star Alliance members are shown in Figure 7.2.

Star Alliance member airlines	
Air Canada	Singapore Airlines
Air New Zealand	South African Airways
ANA	Spanair
Asiana	SWISS
Austrian	TAP Portugal
bmi	Thai Airways International
LOT Polish Airlines	United
Lufthansa	US Airways
SAS	

Figure 7.2 *– Star Alliance member airlines*

Expansion continued with the launch of long-haul British Midland flights to Washington DC in the USA in Spring 2001 and in 2003 the company shortened its name to bmi having already set up bmibaby as a low-cost (budget) airline subsidiary in 2002. In August 2004 bmi carried one million passengers for the first time in a single month. By 2005 bmibaby alone was carrying over 3 million passengers a year, operating 700 flights a week from 5 UK airport bases. The same year saw bmi's first flight from Heathrow to Mumbai in India with further long-haul routes to Riyadh and Jeddah in Saudi Arabia following over the next year. Further domestic and overseas routes continued to be added in 2006-7, including Heathrow to Moscow and Jersey and Edinburgh to Zurich.

Structure

bmi and bmibaby are the brand names under which British Midland Holdings plc, the parent company, provides air transport services to its customers. The corporate headquarters is at Castle Donnington, close to East Midlands airport. bmi remains a Midlands-based business although it operates flights from several UK airport bases, including London Heathrow. The bmi senior management structure is shown in Figure 7.3.

At ownership level, Chairman Sir Michael Bishop owns half of the company, with the remaining shares being held by the two airlines Lufthansa and SAS – Scandinavian Air Services. The executive includes the Chief Executive Officer (CEO) and his Deputy. There are directors for the principal corporate functions of the airline – operations, ground services, IT, finance and engineering, as well as a commercial director and managing directors of bmi (regional) and bmibaby. Senior management posts below board room level include the overall general manager, group treasurer and customer relations manager as well as divisional general managers responsible for cabin services, cargo, charter, and planning and support, as well as a Head of Corporate Communications.

Operations

bmi operates over 1600 flights a week (1200 from London Heathrow) using a fleet of 42 relatively young jet aircraft (on average they are just five years old). Length of journey varies from London-Manchester as the shortest hop to London-Las Vegas as the longest haul. Both scheduled and charter services are provided. The bmi flight network is shown in Figure 7.4.

Since August 2005 bmi has operated a single-class service on its domestic and European services in and out of Heathrow, with a simpler fare structure, internet check-ins (increasingly popular across the domestic/

Executive	Chairman							
	Chief Executive Officer							
	Deputy Chief Executive							
	Chief Operations Officer							
Directorate	Managing Director, bmi Regional	Managing Director, bmibaby	Director, Operations	Director, Ground Services	Director, IT	Director, Engineering	Director, Commercial	Finance Director
Management	General Manager	Group Treasurer	Customer Relations Manager	General Manager, Cabin Services	General Manager, Cargo	General Manager, Charter	General Manager, Planning & Support	Head of Corporate Communications

Figure 7.3 *– bmi senior management structure*

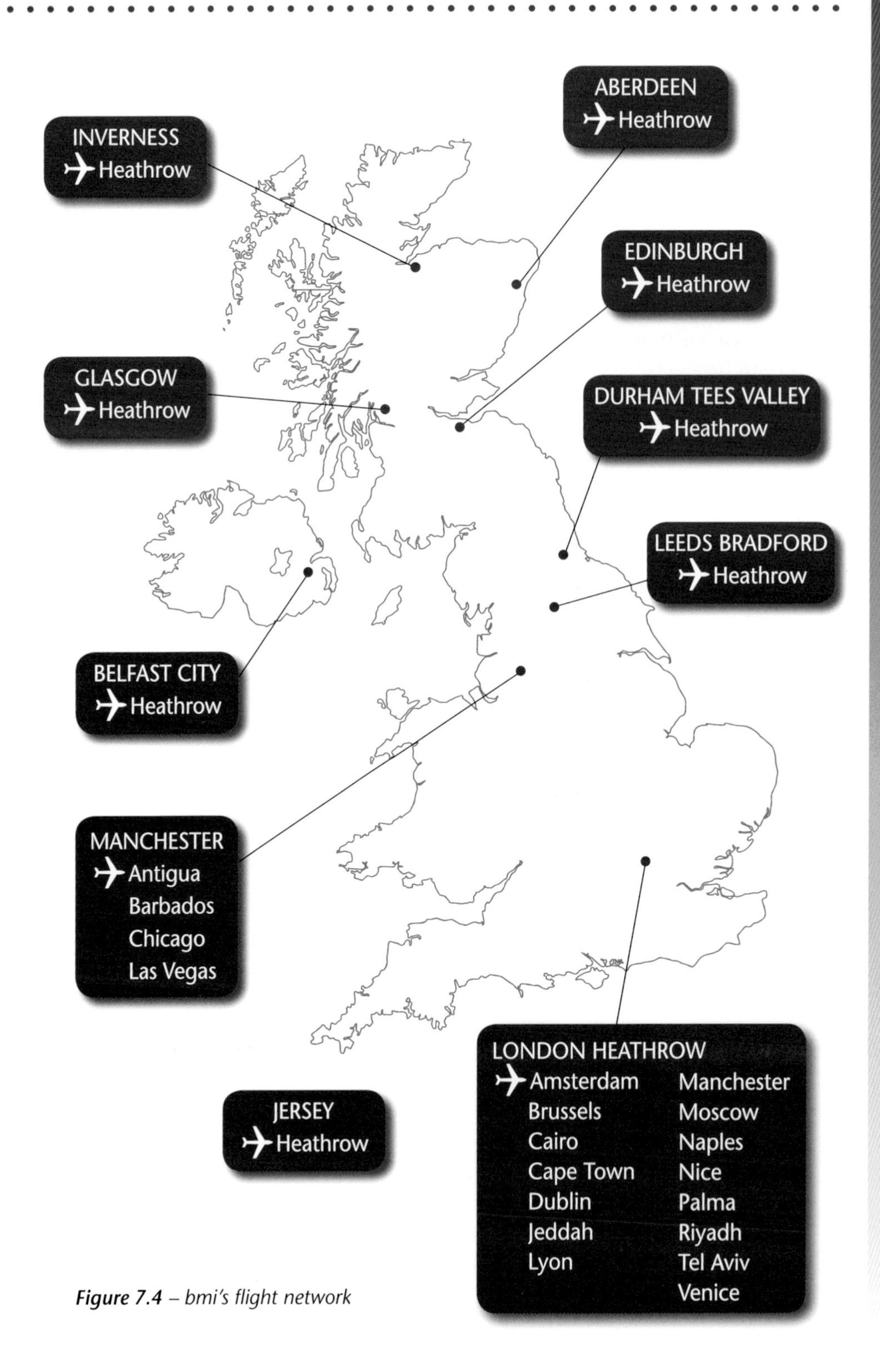

Figure 7.4 – *bmi's flight network*

short-haul airline sector in recent years) and generally quicker processes at airports such as self-service, check-in machines and bag drop facilities. bmi business routes in and out of Heathrow that bmi management sees as core trade – Edinburgh, Glasgow, Belfast, Dublin and Brussels – continue to retain a two-class model with differing levels of cabin service in economy and business class accommodation.

bmi operates flights in co-operation with fellow members of the Star Alliance group of airlines (see Figure 7.2). Further to this, bmi has over 20 'codeshare partners' – other airlines with which it shares flight codes. This means that on a particular flight, the aircraft providing the service may be operated by bmi or by a codeshare partner. Unsurprisingly, bmi's codeshare partners include both Lufthansa and SAS, which between them own half of the company anyway. In addition, more than half of the codeshare partners are Star Alliance members and, conversely, most Star Alliance members are bmi codeshare partners.

Staffing and customer service

bmi employs 4,000 staff, including flight and cabin crew and customer service ground and call centre staff.

Newly-recruited cabin crew and other customer service staff are trained in-house at bmi's own training centre. Training for cabin crew consists of a four-week course, while customer service agents undertake a three-week training period covering customer service skills, and health, safety and security training. Contracts of employment are conditional upon passing the examinations that form the assessment element of these courses.

Applicants, who have responded to advertisements, attended recruitment events or contacted bmi directly, for example via the company's website www.flybmi.com, need to have satisfactory references from previous employers. An aptitude for, and experience of, dealing with people are sought when selecting new staff. The prior acquisition of inter-personal skills is generally valued more highly than technical skills, which include following company procedures. The latter can be taught to newly-recruited staff during training. The inter-personal skills that are needed to serve customers well can and are learned by employees, through training and experience, but they are founded on a base of innate personal qualities such as a cheerful disposition and desire to help people. Interviewees also have to submit to a criminal record check. Those who are successful are notified by the company within a week to ten days of their assessment. Unsuccessful applicants can try again six months later. This is often after gaining some more experience of serving customers.

Finance

bmi's Chairman Sir Michael Bishop is the principal shareholder of the company. He holds 50% if its stock, minus one share. The other half is split between Star Alliance partners Lufthansa and SAS. Lufthansa owns 30% of bmi shares, again less one. Scandinavian Airlines (SAS) initially bought a 24.9% stake in British Midland in 1989, investing a then crucial £25 million, which was a major injection of capital to fund bmi's future development.

bmi's financial results for the tax year ending in 2006, which included bmibaby operations, showed an operating profit of £10.2 million, an increase of 85% on the previous year. Turnover that year was £869 million, up £30 million on the 2004-5 figure and almost £100 million more than in 2003-4. The relative slow down in profits growth may be attributed in part to the particularly warm UK summer of 2006, which impacted negatively on other travel and tourism business (see Case Study 3 on Kuoni, for example). Certainly, the number of bmi passengers remained static at 10.5 million, having risen from 9.4 million between 2003 and 2004.

Marketing

British Midland changed its brand name to bmi in 2003. Establishing a brand name and identity is part of the promotion element of the marketing mix. The new name conveys a marketing message less likely to create a perception of a regionally-based airline than the name British Midland. Its image also comes over as less formal, with a more relaxed but efficient modernity further emphasised by the use of the lower case initials bmi (see Figure 7.5). bmibaby is a separate brand used for the company's low-cost, budget flights.

A further promotion tool for bmi is its frequent flyer Diamond Club loyalty scheme. As with any business, repeat business represents revenue attracted at a lower cost, since the building of brand-awareness and, hopefully of quality perception, has already been achieved. It is therefore to be cherished and worth offering incentives to attract.

Figure 7.5 – bmi's logo

Future

bmi plans further expansion of its fleet and route network. In 2007 the company announced that 10 more aircraft will be added to the fleet in 2008. These will be Airbus A330s and A321s and will cost around £750 million in total.

The company intends to expand its medium-haul network, especially to the Middle East, beginning with the recent launch of a new route from Heathrow to Cairo.

The business's financial strength and diversified portfolio of flights, with feet in both the traditional and low-cost scheduled market camps, suggest a promising future at least in the short to medium-term. The substantial holdings of Lufthansa and SAS, together amounting to 50% of shareholdings, are well established and may be seen as expressions of confidence in bmi's future.

Issues to consider

1. bmi is a member of Star Alliance. Such airline alliances allow passengers the facility (known as interlining) to use the same ticket interchangeably among alliance members.

CONSIDER: How bmi can save costs and raise profits through its membership of the Star Alliance.

2. The Diamond Club is bmi's loyalty reward scheme for frequent flyers.

CONSIDER: Why bmi provides such a scheme for its regular customers.

3. Lufthansa and SAS own 50% of bmi's shares and Sir Michael Bishop the other half (minus one share).

CONSIDER: The advantages and disadvantages to bmi of such an ownership structure.

4. There is growing public awareness of the environmental consequences of air travel.

CONSIDER: (a) The implications for bmi of increased concern about the environmental impact of aviation; (b) The responses airlines such as bmi can make to such concern.

5. Recent years have seen the rapid growth of low-cost airlines. Some observers believe that the differences between low-cost and conventional airlines are lessening to such a degree that there will, in the future, be little to choose between the services each provides.

CONSIDER: What validity there is in such a view and how well the bmi and bmibaby brands are placed to deal with future changes in the air travel market.

6. bmi's routes to destinations such as Russia and the Middle East are being expanded.

CONSIDER: Why bmi management might have chosen to develop the airline's network of routes to these destinations.

Discussion questions

(differentiated by level)

1. bmi and other travel and tourism employers look for appropriate skills and personal qualities when they are recruiting and selecting new staff.

   (a) What is the difference between skills and personal qualities?
   (b) What are the key skills and personal qualities needed by airline cabin crew and customer service agents? (Level 3/GCE AS).

2. Review the bmi logo as a marketing device (Level 3/GCE A2).

3. Compare bmi's senior management structure with that of another UK travel and tourism organisation and comment on the similarities and differences you observe (GCE A2/Foundation Degree).

4. Assess the recent performance of bmi in business terms (Foundation Degree).

british midland
bmi

Virgin Trains

- a rail company

Introduction

Virgin Trains (VT) operates express trains on the West Coast main railway line from London Euston to Birmingham, Manchester, North Wales, Liverpool and Scotland. The company ran trains on a series of cross-country routes in various directions from Birmingham New Street station until it lost the Cross Country franchise in 2007. In the UK, trains are operated by private sector train operating companies (TOCs), like Virgin Trains, along routes that they franchise from the government. The West Coast Main Line is Virgin's remaining franchise.

History and development

Virgin Trains began operating rail passenger services in 1997 on the Cross Country network and on the West Coast Main Line. Virgin replaced existing rolling stock with new Voyager trains on the former in 2001 and with high-speed, electric Pendolino tilting trains on the latter in 2003 (see Figure 8.1). Electric trains like Pendolinos draw their power from overhead electricity cables. They tilt as the train goes around corners at high speed.

To ease ticket purchase, and therefore increase train use and Virgin Trains' turnover, The Trainline online and telephone booking service was

Figure 8.1 – A Virgin Pendolino train (courtesy of ATOC)

launched in 1999 and FastTicket self-service ticket machines introduced at stations in 2000.

Passenger numbers on the cross-country routes operated by Virgin trains since 1997 rose to more than 20 million in 2005, approximately double the figure of ten years previously. In 2007, Virgin's existing two franchises came up for review. The Cross Country franchise was awarded instead to Arriva Trains, but Virgin retained the West Coast Main Line (Figure 8.2).

Structure

Virgin Trains is owned by two shareholders – Virgin Management, led by entrepreneur Sir Richard Branson who owns a majority 51% stake in the business, and bus operator Stagecoach plc, which owns the remaining 49%. These two organisations jointly manage Virgin Trains through a board of directors using the name Virgin Rail Group. Virgin Rail Group has run two train franchise companies as a single entity under an executive team using the Virgin brand. The executive team has consisted of a CEO (Chief Executive Officer), Executive Directors of Commercial Activities and Finance, and two Managing Directors – one for each of the franchises, as well as Sir Richard Branson for Virgin Management and Brian Souter for Stagecoach plc.

***Figure 8.2** – Virgin Trains' West Coast Main Line service*

The Cross Country franchise which Virgin had operated since 1997 was re-franchised by the Department for Transport in 2007 and operated from November that year by Arriva Cross Country. However, the Virgin Trains Cross Country services between Birmingham and Glasgow via Preston were transferred to Virgin Trains West Coast. Cross Country services from Manchester to Scotland, previously operated by Virgin Trains, are now operated by First Trans-Pennine Express. The Virgin Trains West Coast Main Line franchise was renewed in 2007, until 2012.

Operations

Virgin Trains operated almost 400 trains per day in 2007, covering a total distance of 32 million miles and carrying 34 million passengers (94,000 per day). Train operating companies like Virgin Trains operate some stations themselves and share the use of other stations operated by other train companies. Virgin Trains operated 17 of the 113 stations from which the company ran passenger rail services in 2007. It has always been company policy for Virgin Trains to acquire and run new trains – Pendolinos and Voyagers, including Super Voyagers. All the rolling stock Virgin Trains operates is new, completely replacing the old trains that the company inherited from British Rail when the rail industry was privatised. On the West Coast Main Line route, Virgin Trains operates 53 electric, tilting Pendolino trains (including a total of 477 coaches) and in 2007 was running a further 78 Voyager and Super Voyager trains on the Cross Country network.

Since first acquiring its route franchises, Virgin Trains' policy has been to operate new trains equipped with modern safety features. Examples of safety features incorporated into the Virgin Trains' fleet are:

1. Train crumple zones, designed to absorb energy in collisions;

2. Strengthened fuel tanks (to minimise the risk of puncturing and consequent fire);

3. The TPWS (Train Protection Warning System) signal safety system. TPWS reduces the train operating hazard of Signals Passed At Danger (SPADs) by automatically braking if the train driver misses a signal and does not slow down or stop the train.

Virgin Trains operates inter-city passenger train services on the West Coast mainline, which links England, Wales, Scotland and, via the Holyhead to Dun Laoghaire sea crossing, the Republic of Ireland. The principal route is the 400 miles stretch from London Euston to Glasgow Central. From this, tracks branch off to the West Midlands, Liverpool, Manchester and North Wales. Virgin Trains carries about 19 million passengers per year on the West Coast system from and to its 39 stations. The West Coast route is Europe's most used main line.

The permanent way (the railway track itself and its associated signalling and trackside equipment) is the responsibility of Network Rail. Train service providers such as Virgin Trains operate the trains that run along the rail network. Network Rail has undertaken a major modernisation of the track in recent years, with funding from the government. Virgin Trains has continued to operate trains while this project has been underway. Although much of the West Coast Main Line is electrified, allowing the use of Pendolino trains powered from overhead cables, the stretch of line from Crewe to Holyhead is not electrified, so Virgin Trains operates diesel-powered trains including Voyagers.

Staffing and customer service

An overview of The Virgin Trains' staffing picture is shown by Figure 8.3. Of the 4,700 staff employed, 2,900 are on-train staff – just over a thousand drivers and 1800 other train crew, including train and onboard shop managers and first class coach stewards. 860 staff work at stations as customer service and train dispatch personnel.

On-train staff	2,900
On-station staff	860
Drivers	108
Administration, etc.	832
Total staff	**4,700**

Figure 8.3 *– Staffing at Virgin Trains*

Staff training and development programmes are intended to ensure the delivery of high quality customer service as well as the safe operation of Virgin trains. All VT drivers, for example, undergo training at the two Virgin Trains' driver training centres in Crewe:

- The Driver Simulation Centre, which has three full-size train cab simulators replicating Virgin's Pendolino, Voyager and Super Voyager trains. For Pendolino tilting train drivers, training has included the operation of the Tilt Authorisation Speed Supervision (TASS) system;
- The VT Computer-based Training Centre, which is equipped with interactive computer work stations, where train drivers learn and practise correct procedures.

Virgin has a continuing need for newly-trained drivers as a result of natural staff wastage. Initial driver training is in small groups (up to 10 trainee drivers at a time). It takes more than a year to complete the training. Prior to the initial training course, trainee drivers undergo medical and reaction time assessments. During initial training, drivers learn about the rules and procedures required to operate trains safely, as well as finding out how the trains work, plus acquiring the necessary skills to operate them correctly. As part of the programme, trainee drivers are allocated to a Virgin Trains' depot to gain practical driving experience under the supervision of a qualified instructor. At the end of the course there are tests (theory and practical) to be passed before starting full-time train driving. Some trainee drivers are recruited from the rail transport provider sector, perhaps having worked onboard Virgin trains in a customer service role or at a station, for example as a train dispatcher. Most VT driver trainees, however, are new to Virgin and to rail transport work.

The two VT driver training centres are not used just for initial driver training. Virgin's drivers return to the Crewe centres to receive refresher and top-up training as well as for further skills development using the simulators and computer-based training systems. This is part of VT's driver competence development system.

Onboard a Virgin train, the train manager is in charge of the passenger accommodation, checking tickets and looking after the safety and comfort of customers as well as supervising colleagues. A shop is provided for first and standard class passengers to use, selling refreshments, magazines and headphones to use with the onboard audio system. First class passengers are provided with an at-seat refreshment service.

On stations, train dispatch staff oversee the safe departure of trains and act as information sources for passengers. Stations that Virgin Trains operates have first class lounges for the exclusive use of Virgin Trains' first class passengers, offering complimentary drinks and quiet, comfortable waiting environments.

To facilitate the use of its trains by all its customers, and to comply with the Rail Vehicle Accessibility Regulations 1998 and with the Disability Discrimination Act 1995, Virgin's trains incorporate a variety of special features:

- At least one dedicated accommodation space for a wheelchair with a call-for-aid button to contact train staff;
- Wider doors to ease access to trains from platforms, although the inevitable step up to the train and gap between it and the platform continue to present obstacles that can be overcome by the use of wheelchair ramps;
- Wheelchair-accessible toilets, with enhanced specifications including a larger floor area than standard conveniences;
- Brail signage to assist visually-impaired customers;
- Audible and visual information systems, for example voice announcements alerting passengers that the train is approaching a station are backed up by a digital display in each coach.

Virgin has also addressed access issues at the 17 stations it operates on the West Coast Main Line, with easier-to-reach ticket counters and improved information systems. Wheelchair-accessible toilets are also provided along with passenger lifts to make it easier for passengers to cross, with their luggage, from one station platform to another.

Customers with special needs may expect that they will need some assistance from Virgin Trains' staff during their journey – at the station, on the train, or both. Such passengers are encouraged to arrange for some help at the time they book their tickets. They can do this by telephoning or texting Virgin Trains' JourneyCare dedicated special needs customer service unit (customers who find voice telephones difficult often use textphones). VT JourneyCare staff can then make forward arrangements to ease the passenger's journey and limit the train's station dwell time (the length of time the train stands at a platform between arriving at and departing from a station) to try to keep it running on time. Virgin Trains' management also encourage staff to help customers who have special needs, but have not made special arrangements in advance, whenever

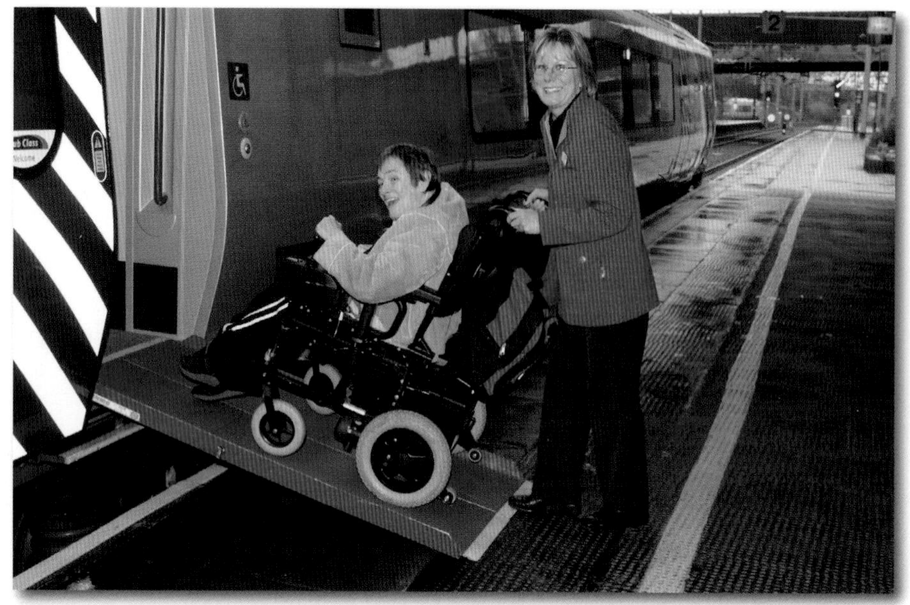

Figure 8.4 – *Passenger assistance on a Virgin train*

they can. However, staff have to remember that their first responsibility is for the health and safety of themselves, the passengers and other staff. This can sometimes limit the help they can provide at short notice.

Like other transport providers, train operating companies such as Virgin Trains publish a Passenger's Charter. This gives customers information about the service that Virgin Trains intends to provide for them before, during and after each journey. It also gives details of compensation arrangements if things go wrong. When customer service quality or train performance falls short of the standards outlined in the Passenger's Charter, Virgin Trains is obliged to take appropriate action, as outlined in the Charter.

The provisions of the Virgin Trains' Passenger's Charter include the organisation's undertakings to:

- Provide impartial information to customers about journey planning and about ticket prices;
- Meet the needs of customers with disabilities;
- Inform customers who are not satisfied with Virgin Trains response to an issue or complaint that they can write to Passenger Focus – an independent body established by the Government to protect the interests of rail passengers.

The VT Passenger's Charter does not create any contractual, legal relationship between Virgin Trains and its customers. The company's legal obligations are set down in the National Rail Conditions of Carriage. These conditions form part of the customer's contract with Virgin Trains when s/he buys a ticket. They apply to all train operating companies in the UK.

Finance and funding

Virgin Trains' turnover was £579 million in 2006. With track access charges to pay to Network Rail of £526 million (agreed under the franchise arrangement) and leasing costs for the trains themselves of nearly £300 million, a government subsidy of £526 million was clearly necessary support to ensure continued operation and investment.

Virgin Trains, in common with other train operators, does not own the trains it runs, but leases them from train providers Alstom Transportation and Angel Trains who own the Pendolino electric tilting train fleet.

Marketing

'Return of the Train' has been a Virgin Trains' promotional theme in recent months. The introduction of new rolling stock with sleek modern designs on the upgraded West Coast Main Line presented Virgin Trains with the opportunity to re-launch rail travel and win passengers from the road and domestic air travel sectors. The theme of modernity is continued through the company's relatively informal staff uniform and customer service style, bright red livery, a shop rather than buffet and electronic reserved seat displays. Prior to introducing Virgin Trains, Virgin Atlantic was already established in the air travel market so it made sense to present a rail service that potential customers would recognise from that successful brand. Apart from the retention of the red livery and Virgin logo, the introduction of airline style features such as audio headphones and, to begin with, a club rather than first premium class fitted in with Sir Richard Branson's vision of a rail service informed by passengers' expectations of air travel.

Price is a crucial marketing mix element in balancing the use of trains between peak times (when trains can become very full and passengers may have to stand) and slack periods. The internet marketing of tickets combines pricing policy with place by allowing passengers to see a range of price options and times for their journeys. First class upgrades are also offered as a way of marketing Virgin's premium first class service.

Virgin Trains trades on the whole Virgin brand's relatively informal image. The Virgin Group of companies hold key brand values including innovation and fun. Particularly to catch the attention of younger potential customers (many students use Virgin trains for example), the company has made use of the viral marketing technique. The idea of viral marketing is to manipulate the informal word-of-mouth marketing that happens anyway among any organisation's customers – actual and potential. A short, quirky video-clip, for instance, can stimulate potential customers to talk about the company and see it in a positive light – grist to the mill of the marketer. In 2007, Virgin Trains commissioned a comedy video clip about global warming issues. This was initially used as a television advertisement, but subsequently found its way onto the internet (You Tube, for example). The short film used actors dressed as countryside creatures to humorously plug the company's low carbon footprint. Content was pitched so that the commercial would be a discussion point among young, environmentally-conscious potential customers. They would start talking to each other about the clip and about Virgin Trains and, would, as a result, be more likely to buy Virgin Trains' tickets.

Future

Virgin's plan for the future of the West Coast Main Line is to develop a high-speed and frequent rail service, with further reduced journey times between cities along the route. To this end, Virgin Trains co-operates with other transport providers including Alstom Transportation, Angel Trains and Network Rail, which is responsible for the track and infrastructure.

In 2012, Virgin Trains' franchise will come up for renewal again and Virgin Trains will, if it chooses, need to mount a new bid to retain it. Other transport providers may compete, as happened when Arriva was successful in outbidding Virgin for the Cross Country franchise in 2007. Virgin Trains may decide to bid for other rail route franchises as they are opened up to bidders.

The West Coast Main Line on which Virgin Trains operates is largely electrified, allowing the use of tilting, Pendolino trains. However, Virgin Trains is currently obliged to run diesel Voyager trains between Crewe and

Holyhead because this spur has not been electrified. Diesel locomotives emit more than twice as much carbon dioxide as electric trains. As the UK government moves to cut the country's carbon emissions during the 21st century, electrification of the whole inter-city rail network would make a substantial contribution towards a sustainable transport system in the future. However, Network Rail has calculated that the cost of doing so would be £500,000 per kilometre, meaning, for example, that to electrify the main line between London and Bristol would cost £380 million. This is such an economic disincentive that sections such as the Crewe-Holyhead stretch are likely to continue to be served by diesel trains as far ahead as 2045, emitting up to 112g of CO2 per passenger kilometre, compared to as little as 28g/pkm for the most efficient electric trains.

Issues to consider

1. Franchise agreements, under which train operators run services, have to be renewed periodically. It is by no means automatic that the incumbent operator will retain its franchise in the face of competition from other bidders. In 2007, for example, Virgin Trains was unsuccessful in its bid to retain the Cross Country franchise, which was won by Arriva Trains.

   CONSIDER: The effects of the UK rail franchise system on (a) the Virgin Trains' business; (b) the quality of rail transport services.

2. There is growing concern among the travelling public about the environmental impact of transport. Trains are considered to be less of a problem than aircraft.

   CONSIDER: The opportunities presented to Virgin Trains of growing environmental concerns.

3. Overcrowding on some services means that some passengers, who may have paid over £100 for a ticket, must sometimes stand.

   CONSIDER: The threat posed to Virgin Trains of overcrowded services and suggest how Virgin management might seek to minimise it.

4. The UK government provides a subsidy to Virgin Trains, as it does to other train operating companies (TOCs), to help them operate their services. The terms for repaying this money are part of the franchise agreement between VT and the Department for Transport.

CONSIDER: Whether the UK government should subsidise private companies like Virgin Trains to operate trains on the country's passenger rail network.

5. Railway tickets currently remain largely in paper form. Many airlines no longer issue paper tickets at all. The technology for selling electronic tickets, for example by text to mobile 'phone users with a bar code that can be read by automatic ticket barriers, is under development.

CONSIDER: How appropriate it would be for a TOC such as Virgin Trains to provide ticketless travel.

Discussion questions

(differentiated by level)

1. Compare the advantages and disadvantages for different customer types of using Virgin Trains West Coast Main Line rail services to those of other means of travelling between the north-west of England and a major London airport (Level 3/GCE AS).

2. Suggest how a train operator such as Virgin Trains can use 'place' to help market its products and services (Level 3/GCE A2).

3. How do the environmental impacts of rail, coach and air travel within the UK compare? (Level 3/GCE A2).

4. Assess the benefits to travel in the UK of the rail franchise system (Foundation Degree).

9

Shearings

– a coach tour operator

Introduction

Shearings Holidays is a major UK tour operator specialising in coach holidays, aimed primarily at older people – the so called 'grey market'. The company offers holidays in the UK and overseas. Shearings is a diversified business providing cruise and air travel holidays as well as coach-based trips. As well as 300 coaches, the company's assets include a chain of 44 hotels and 8 high street travel agency shops. For 2008, as Figure 9.1 shows, a range of four different Shearings Holidays brochures promoted the company's products:

- Explore UK and Ireland;
- Discover Europe;
- Cruise Europe;
- Classic Hotels.

Figure 9.1 – Holiday products offered by Shearings

History and development

Shearings Holidays is the current name for the company that was previously called WA Shearings (WAS), the business formed in 2005 by the merger of Coach Holiday Group (owners of Wallace Arnold) and Shearings. It is Europe's largest coach tour operator and has a long history. Wallace Arnold, named after its founders, was established in Leeds as long ago as 1912. Wallace Arnold was the leading British package coach tour company in its mid to late 20th century heyday. The company was a pioneer of this type of holiday and operated tours throughout the UK at a time when car ownership, especially among its target mature adult market, was relatively low. Smith Shearing, the other half of the merged business, has always been based in Wigan where the current company headquarters is located.

Structure

Shearings head office is in Wigan. Reservations, whether made directly by telephone or via the company website www.shearings.com, or through high street retail travel agents, are collated in Wigan. The company also operates a small chain of 8 travel shops located in Yorkshire and Derbyshire, for example in Bradford, Rotherham and Chesterfield.

Operations

Shearings Holidays' core business is in operating coach tours, in the UK, the Irish Republic and continental Europe. In the British Isles, their destinations include London, traditional seaside resorts such as Newquay and Great Yarmouth, countryside areas such as Galway in Ireland and heritage destinations like Stratford-upon-Avon. Shearings also operate coach holidays to 17 different countries on the continent.

Shearings coaches are fitted to three specifications – the British Tour Coach (see Figure 9.2) with 46 seats, plus the Euro Tourer and Grand Tourer coaches, which have 42 and 36 seats respectively, thereby offering customers more space and leg room.

Figure 9.2 – The British Tour Coach

Different strategies are used to collect each coach party prior to driving to a destination. Customers in densely-populated areas can opt for Shearings 'Home Connect Service'. For a supplementary charge, Shearings collect customers from their own homes by minibus and transfer them to the main coach departure point. Other strategies Shearings use are their 'Tour Connect' service and 'Direct Connect'. The former involves customers meeting a Shearings coach at a convenient location such as their local town centre. They are then transferred, along with other Shearings' customers, who may be going on different tours, to a central tour departure point. Tours are operated with regional starting points, such as motorway service stations, to facilitate this process. 'Direct Connect' is when customers arrange their own transport to a main coach departure point.

Some tours include accommodation at one of the hotels Shearings operates in 37 UK locations, mostly on the coast and in the Scottish Highlands and Borders. Many tours use Shearings' own coaches, but some, for example to London and the South East, use coaches belonging to other, partner coach operators.

Shearings also operate air travel, rail tours and cruises. Some tours to Ireland and the north of Scotland include flights either as an alternative to travelling to a distant tour area by coach or as an integral part of the itinerary. Cruise tours are combined with coach travel, for example the round-Britain 'British Discovery' cruise with coach travel to and from Dover, or with air travel, for example for cruising the Scottish Highlands and Islands.

Staffing and customer service

Shearings employs approximately 3,000 people and serves a customer base of around three million, mostly in the over-50 age group. About a million passengers travel with the company annually. Repeat business and business generated as a result of recommendations shared by target market members are vital to the profitable operation of Shearings. Customer feedback is actively gathered so that management can monitor levels of customer satisfaction and make any necessary adjustments to products and services.

To help maintain customer confidence and service quality, Shearings is a member of CoachMarque, set up by the Confederation of Passenger Transport (CPT), the trade association representing Britain's bus, coach and light rail operators. CoachMarque provides a measurable standard for the buyers of coach transport, who may be groups and organisations as well as individuals. It is the only standards accreditation scheme devised by the travel industry for other industry organisations to use. Consumers can also gain a clearer picture of what standards they can expect from UK coach providers. All CoachMarque members, including Shearings, are independently audited to prove they comply with the CoachMarque quality standards, which are listed in Figure 9.3.

A number of CPT members, Shearings included, additionally belong to a consumer travel protection scheme called Bonded Coach Holidays (BCH), which is approved by the Department of Trade and Industry as satisfying the requirements of the European Union Package Travel Regulations. Customers who book a holiday covered by the scheme have protection for the money they paid for their holiday, in the event of the company going out of business before departure, and for completion of their holiday

- The Company will have an appointed person within the organisation to be responsible for all the health and safety issues.
- It will have a comprehensive health and safety policy available for inspection.
- It will have a policy of informing customers of the on-board safety procedures before departure.
- Drivers licences are checked on a regular basis to ensure that drivers have a current valid licence for the type of vehicle they are likely to drive.
- An approved and documented training policy is in place.
- All drivers will have a copy of a drivers' handbook containing relevant information required to carry out their duties professionally and in line with company policy.
- The Company fully complies with all the necessary insurance requirements for public liability, group vehicle cover, employers insurance and, where appropriate, tour operator liability.
- Where appropriate, the Company will comply fully with current legislation concerning package travel, including safeguarding client's money paid in advance.
- The Company will provide a 24-hour helpline to be used in cases of emergency.
- All CoachMarque accredited vehicles will be under 10 years old, comply with the latest European safety standards, which require a crush proof safety cell in the case of rollover accident, and are fitted with speed limiters.
- All vehicles will be subject to a rigorous preventative maintenance programme to maximise reliability and safety.
- The Company will operate from an identifiable operating base.
- The driver will be in full uniform.
- The coach will be presented in a clean and safe condition and be fitted with seat belts.
- Vehicles will be equipped with mobile communications.
- In the unlikely event of a complaint, the Company operates a formal procedure to deal effectively and quickly with any client dissatisfaction.

***Figure 9.3** – The CoachMarque standards for coach operators*

or return home if such an eventuality occurs while they are actually on the holiday. Because Shearings' customers are largely from the 50+ age bracket – an age group with a reputation for taking particular care over money matters – such a bonding scheme is an important and reassuring marketing device. Consequently, both the BCH and CoachMarque logos appear on Shearings' promotional materials, including their brochures and website.

Finance

Shearings has annual sales of £200 million. In 2006 the company arranged for re-financing worth £25 million from Lloyds TSB bank and £78 million from the sale and leaseback of 39 of its hotels. The Lloyds TSB arrangement included a £5 million foreign exchange dealing service to limit the risk to Shearings' business of sudden fluctuations in fuel prices and international currency markets. These two re-financing deals came the year after the £200 million merger between Shearings and the owners of Wallace Arnold, funded by venture capital firm 3i, which left Shearings in significant debt.

3i had calculated that the merged Coach Holidays Group and Shearings business would have the opportunity to make savings of up to £24 million by eliminating operation duplications. In addition, more choice could be offered to customers because of the increased size of the combined business. The deal to sell 39 of its UK hotels to property investment firm Moorfield Group has allowed Shearings to pay off much of its debt and take advantage of the opportunities 3i had seen.

Shearings continues to operate the hotels, many of which are in seaside resorts, for example the Norbreck and New Southlands hotels in Scarborough, and the Royal in Whitby. The company's management has signed long-term leases on the hotels over which it has full operational control. Such separation of asset ownership and operation has become increasingly common in the hotel sector in recent years with Travelodge, Hilton, Thistle and Accor all engaging in similar arrangements.

Marketing

To help business planning, Shearings' management commission market research into trends within their key market segment – 'mature' tourists. Recent findings have shown that UK breaks are more popular than foreign holidays for the over-45s, with customers aged between 45 and 55 taking more breaks than any other age group in the UK and one in ten taking more than four short breaks a year – nearly double the national figure of 6.9%. People in this age bracket also take more city breaks than any other. Market research has also found that long weekends become increasingly important to people as they age, with 13% aged 65+ choosing a long weekend break – 5% more than those aged 55-64 and almost double the national average of 7%.

Stereotypical perceptions of the demands of 'grey market' members can be misleading. One in 12 of travellers aged over 65 are choosing to go on adventure and activity holidays. Just 36% of them are primarily seeking relaxation on holiday – less than every other age group except 16-24 year olds (33%). A third of over-55s book holidays online, but, on the other hand, 37% still prefer to book through travel agents.

While the highest-spending holidaymakers are aged 35-44, with 32% spending more than £2,000, the average spend for those aged between 45-54 is £1,494, dropping to £1,352 for those aged 55-65 and to £1,074 for those over 65. However, this is still significantly more than the average £952 spent by 16-24 year olds on their annual holiday.

Keenly aware of Shearings' dependence on the 50+ market, management moved to allay anxieties and concerns expressed by customers following the 2005 merger. Repeat business represents about 80% of Shearings' annual turnover. Some customers have been travelling with the firm for 20 years, so the top marketing priority was to ensure that they were reassured that prices would not rise and choice and the quality of the holiday experience would not suffer as a result of Shearings and Wallace Arnold merging. The retention of long–established customers was crucial not only for generating their repeat business, but also for the extra custom they can bring from friends and acquaintances they talk to. Such 'word-of-mouth' marketing is free and very effective, provided that customers speak well of the company. Negative comments can be very destructive in the market place.

Even in the 'grey market', e-marketing matters. Market research has shown Shearings' managers that a third of tourists aged 55+ book holidays and travel products online. Following the merger of Wallace Arnold and Shearings Holidays in 2005, the newly-enlarged company has benefited from a new, common website which is quicker and easier to navigate than either of its predecessors. Improved technology has allowed Shearings to link the company's brochure content with the website so that users can search availability online. Shearings worked with IT partner organisation Modcomp to get brochure content onto the website and allow availability search. Data from Shearings' reservations database is extracted on a daily basis and imported to the server database online. Users are consequently able to check availability for holidays from the current brochures in as near to real time as possible. A second content database has been developed to provide a source for further information on each holiday or destination, which users can access as they search availability. A communication link between Shearings' website and the company's reservations centre in Wigan allows users to make a provisional booking online or to request a telephone call back from the staff reservations team.

Future

The increased scale of the business following the 2005 merger puts Shearings in a powerful position in what is a stable sector of the UK holiday market – coach holiday provision for older adults. The company management plans to grow the business further, using capital from the 2006 re-financing to invest in the brand to lead provision for an increasingly affluent market segment. As the population of the UK ages and as more 'grey market' members have wealth accumulated from property ownership and life assurance schemes, Shearings can expect increasing demand and levels of spend to come its way. Around 40% of the UK population is now aged over 50 and they own 80% of the country's wealth.

Shearings has signed long-term leases on the hotels it has sold, so that it will not only have full operational control over these assets in the future, but will also command a £25m capital investment programme into the next decade. Management see this as important for ensuring that Shearings can set accommodation quality standards in line with the benchmarks it sets for the other elements of the customer experience.

Travel agent training by Shearings may be stepped up to counter what its management see as a misplaced view that coach tours are cheap, tame holidays for people who are much older than 50. Active itineraries for 50 and 60-somethings are increasingly popular with customers. The now expanded range of European 'fly-coach' holidays may also be further widened.

Shearings' management team and private equity investor partners 3i intend to make use of 3i's network of other venture capital investments to work with other organisations to develop new products for the company to attract new customers. The 55 year olds of the future will have demands that are very different from the 55 year olds of now, who already seek different travel experiences than the 55 year olds of just a few years ago.

Issues to consider

1. Sudden fluctuations can occur in both fuel prices and international currency exchange rates.

CONSIDER: The extent to which Shearings' business is at risk from such shifts.

2. Shearings management believes that travel agents have been slow to sell coaching holidays compared to cruises despite the coach tours' market being double the size.

CONSIDER: Why travel agents may be more active in the cruising holiday market than in the selling of coach holidays.

3. Coach holidays have an image of catering mainly for older passengers.

CONSIDER: The extent to which this issue should matter to Shearings.

4. The UK coach tours' sector is worth about £2 billion. It is less volatile than the holiday market as a whole, but it is also highly fragmented with over 600 operators involved.

CONSIDER: What opportunities and threats the nature of the coach tours' market presents for Shearings.

5. Environmentally friendly holidays are increasingly popular.

CONSIDER: How Shearings could present itself to the market as an environmentally-friendly operator.

Discussion questions

(differentiated by level)

1. (a) Explain why coach holidays have, since at least the 1960s, appealed mostly to older customers (Level 3/GCE AS).

   (b) Suggest how Shearings might go about attracting a younger clientele (Level 3/GCE A2).

2. The management of Shearings believes that travel agents have been slow to sell coaching holidays, despite the size of the market and earnings potential: "The trade is in touch with cruising and places importance on it, yet coaching, which is double the size, is seen as 'niche' and less glamorous". Discuss the truth of this contention and examine how Shearings might counteract travel agents' perceived reluctance to sell its products (Level 3/GCE A2).

3. How can Shearings' management try to insulate the business from volatility in fuel prices and sudden swings in currency exchange rates (Foundation Degree).

10

Novotel

– a hotel provider

Introduction

Novotel is a hotel brand belonging to the Accor group of companies, which is, in turn, a global provider of hotel accommodation. Other Accor hotel brands include Formule 1, Etap, Ibis, Mercure and Sofitel. Accor pitches its brands at different levels of the market range; Formule 1, for example, is a cheaper, budget brand, while Sofitel is at the luxury end of the market.

Accor's target market for the Novotel brand is the mid to upper level of the market range. The Novotel concept is of an international chain of modern, practical and informal hotels catering for both business and leisure tourists. Globally, there are 396 Novotel hotels in 58 countries. The UK currently has 31 Novotel hotels.

Novotel hotels are generally located in three distinct areas:

- City centres, for example Leeds and London St. Pancras;
- At or near airports, for example Newcastle and Birmingham Airport;
- In suburbs, often on business/retail parks or at transport nodes, for example Plymouth and Nottingham/Derby.

History/development

The business was founded in France by Paul Dubrule and Gérard Pelisson. The first Novotel was opened in 1967 at Lille Lesquin in north-eastern France. The core idea behind the brand from the outset was to provide purpose-built, modern, comfortable hotel accommodation, coupled with restaurants, work and recreational facilities, plus car parking. Following the establishment of the first Ibis hotel (in Bordeaux) in 1974, the company, then called SIEH, bought the Mercure (in 1975) and Sofitel (in 1980) hotel chains and became Accor in 1983. In 2005 the Novotel Madrid Sanchinarro opened as Accor's 4000th hotel.

Novotel developments aim to adapt to customers' changing lifestyles. Its recently-introduced 'Novation' bedrooms are a deliberate tactic aimed at keeping up with consumer trends to maintain the perception of freshness and modernity, which is key to the Novotel brand image.

***Figure 10.1** – Bedroom at a 'new generation' Novotel*

Structure

Accor began with Novotel, but the group has dealt in a variety of business interests, not only hotels. For example, it owned the Carlson Wagonlit business travel agency chain until 2006. Its business interests have also expanded outside the travel and tourism industry, for example the American employment services firm Worklife Benefits, which Accor merged with Workplace Options in 2005. The global group business structure has been highly diversified, but in 2007 it moved to concentrate on its two key business areas:

- Hotels;
- Tourism support services.

The Accor brand structure in the UK hotels sector is shown in Figure 10.2. Of the Accor brands, Novotel hotels are second only to Ibis hotels in terms of strength of UK presence and the Novotel brand is widely perceived by consumers as the upmarket sibling of Ibis. In some locations, Manchester city centre for example, the two separately branded hotels are next-door neighbours.

Brand	Market range	UK presence
Sofitel	Up ↑	3 luxury hotels, all in the London area
Novotel		31 hotels
Mercure		26 hotels, re-branded in 2007
Ibis		49 hotels
Etap		11 hotels
Formule 1	↓ Down	5 budget hotels

Figure 10.2 *– Accor hotels UK brand structure*

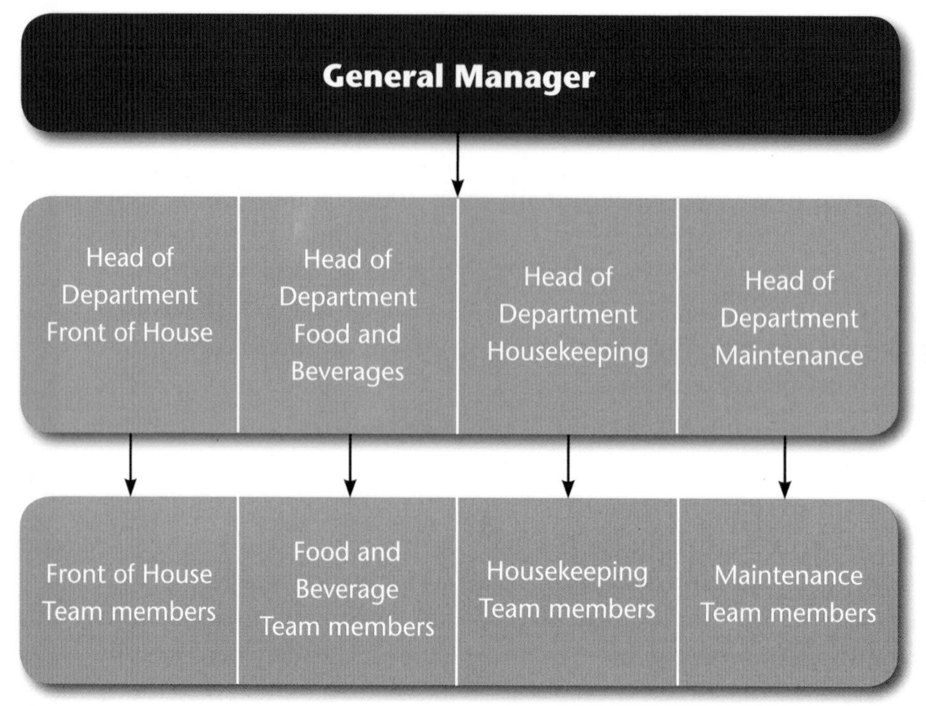

Figure 10.3 *– Novotel UK hotel management structure*

Figure 10.3 shows the management structure of a typical Novotel in the UK. It is a fairly 'flat' structure, with staff working as a team on a relatively equal basis. Nevertheless, there are hierarchical elements; the General Manager is in charge of the hotel and is responsible for the work of the Department Managers who in turn manage the members of their own teams. The larger Novotel UK hotels have more management team members, a Rooms Manager for instance, and an Operations Manager to deputise, as necessary, for the General Manager.

Operations

Accor operate 31 Novotel hotels in the UK, each with a restaurant, bar, leisure facilities, en-suite bedrooms and meeting rooms for business guests, whether resident or not. Most hotels have a car park and one in two has a swimming pool. Catering for family guests, bed settees are provided and inter-connecting rooms are available in some hotels. Wi-fi internet access, via Orange France, is made available at a supplementary charge.

The Novotel London St. Pancras is one example of the Novotel brand in the UK. Previously the Novotel London Euston, the hotel was renamed in 2007 when the nearby St. Pancras International railway station, just 3 minutes from the hotel, became the London terminal for Eurostar trains to the Continent. Novotel London St. Pancras is a 4-star hotel, comprising 312 bedrooms and suites, Mirrors restaurant and bar, 16 conference rooms and a fitness centre. Room service is provided 24 hours a day.

Customer service and staffing

Novotel hotels in the UK have introduced a customer service concept called 'Service Extraordinaire', emphasising the company's French roots. 'Service Extraordinaire' simply means extraordinary service. It is a training programme aimed at enabling hotel staff to provide excellent customer service, with an edge over Novotel's competitors, an edge that the Novotel UK senior management team refers to as 'The Novotel Difference'. The first Novotel to introduce 'Service Extraordinaire' was Novotel London West in 2003. That year Novotel London West won the Best Training Team of the Year award for Service Excellence in the National Consumer Service Awards.

Novotel management, making use of market research findings, defines the customer service it wants its guests to receive as:

- A hassle-free stay;
- Staff who are proactive in meeting customer needs;
- Customers who feel comfortable and relaxed;
- Customers who have a choice over the service they receive;
- Service that is delivered with a human touch.

'Service Extraordinaire' was introduced to Novotel's staff as a way of enhancing the already good customer service they were delivering. The Novotel UK vision is to be the brand of choice for its customers and for its employees. If Novotel UK can attract the best staff, because they want to work for the company, customer service is likely to improve still further and staff turnover will be reduced.

Novotel organises training for staff, in the hotel where they normally work, by colleagues they already know. All staff are trained in Novotel

UK's four hotel standards and seven service behaviours, as shown in Figure 10.4. Training is delivered through:

- Awareness-raising – staff meetings, posters and newsletters are used to familiarise staff with the four hotel standards (Figure 10.4);
- Induction to 'Service Extraordinaire' – all staff attend a 3-hour induction to the 'Service Extraordinaire' training course;
- A 2-day seminar;
- Follow-up training by 'hotel coaches' (see below).

'Hotel coaches' are in-house trainers within a Novotel hotel. They need not be senior members of the hotel management, but simply be well-established members of the staff team who have a particular interest in customer service quality and an aptitude for training colleagues. Hotel coaches are able to pass on comments to new staff that help colleagues keep up the four hotel standards, without it seeming like a reprimand from a manager. For example, one of the standards is to 'look professional'. A team member who is seen to be not looking as smart as usual in a simple way such as not having their tie correctly fastened or being as well-groomed as usual, may feel less threatened to have this pointed out by a peer rather than by a senior manager.

Figure 10.4 *– 'Service Extraordinaire' customer service criteria*

To monitor the quality of 'Service Extraordinaire' customer service standards, Novotel hotel managers use a variety of tools that include:

- The qualisurvey;
- The floor-walk;
- The image check-up.

The qualisurvey involves face-to-face interviews being held with hotel guests, typically 5 or 6, every day. A senior staff member, such as the General Manager, approaches guests in the hotel lobby and asks them to take part. Most are happy to do so. They sit down together and talk through the guest's experience of Novotel.

Staff undertaking this task are senior personnel who have received training in dealing with customer complaints. It is important that the guest feels able to share anything that has not lived up to their expectations without the staff member seeming offended by this. The General Manager is keen to discover any downsides to the customer service that guests have received. From a company perspective, it is much better that even minor dissatisfactions are known. If Novotel is not aware of problems, they cannot be rectified and business may be damaged because of people being put off for unknown reasons. Feedback from the guest interviews is discussed at each morning's management meeting.

The floor-walk is a daily event. A senior member of staff, or the hotel coach, walks around the hotel. The floor-walker checks each of the hotel's departments. In the case of a typical UK Novotel these may be front of house, food and beverage, housekeeping and maintenance. Customer service delivery and staff grooming standards are observed and reported to each Head of Department.

The image check-up consists of management team members carrying out random observations of telephone answering, e-mail and fax-sending to monitor the standard of communication with customers outside the hotel. The qualisurvey and floor-walk measure customer service quality inside the hotel.

Other quality measures include guest rooms' customer comment cards. Every time a room is prepared for new customers one of these cards is left. The customer can hand in their comments confidentially on check-out or post them to Accor later. Daily management meetings are held with Department Heads and the General Manager or his/her deputy. Issues raised by any of the quality survey measures are dealt with immediately.

Financial strategy

Senior management in Accor have decided to concentrate on the core businesses of hotels and tourism support services, because they believe this will increase overall profits and the dividends they can pay to shareholders. Financial results indicate that this strategy appears to be successful.

The Accor Group's finances have strengthened and shown real growth in recent years. The operating profit in 2006, for instance, was up 28% on the previous year's figure to 727million Euros (approximately £525 million). The Novotel brand is in the mid to upper market segment where Accor's profits have been particularly high, some 60% higher than for economy brands (Formule 1 and Etap in the UK).

Marketing

Customer service quality is in itself an important element in Novotel's marketing strategy. Having a well-regarded hotel service product is important to Novotel not only for the retention of existing customers but also to attract new guests. This is achieved through the mechanism of 'below-the-line' communication – the hidden marketing of word-of-mouth whereby a past or present customer passes on to other potential customers a hopefully positive recommendation of the hotel chain. Not only does this process lead to more business and increase the company's turnover, but it also comes at no extra financial cost beyond delivering the product well. The effectiveness of Novotel's 'Service Extraordinaire' programme is therefore enhanced and the financial and human resources investment in it further justified by the marketing spin-off it generates.

E-marketing (electronic marketing) is another approach used by Novotel, as it is by other Accor brands, to attract repeat business. Many customers now book online, using the Novotel or Accor websites. Novotel does not find it necessary to enter into partnership with an online booker such as Expedia (Case Study 6), for example. Unless they have indicted otherwise, customers receive regular e-mailings to keep up the level of their awareness of the Novotel brand and attract them by means of special offers on stays at selected hotels. A business customer may be enticed to make a leisure booking as well as further business bookings and trade volume grows as a result.

In 2006 the Accor Group's management re-examined the Novotel brand's marketing strategy and decided on raising its advertising profile alongside that of its Ibis brand. As a result, a Europe-wide advertising campaign was launched as a more direct appeal to customers who, it was felt, needed a reminder about the benefits of staying at a Novotel. Like many other hotel chains, Novotels are ubiquitous across the cities of Europe and so much a part of the accepted scene that they were seen to be at risk of blending into the background. Renewed advertising was seen as a means of counteracting this.

Figure 10.5 *– The distinctive Novotel logo*

Future

The 'Service Extraordinaire' programme of enhanced customer service, designed to make 'the Novotel difference' a real competitive edge over the company's rival hotel providers, has been introduced gradually to the company's UK hotels since 2003. In the immediate future, this rolling programme is set to continue to expand across the brand. Expanded capacity is also planned with a £2 billion capital investment plan for the period 2006-2010 already underway. Management intends to spend about £300 million acquiring hotels and £1.5 billion on expansion to open 200,000 new rooms.

Issues to consider

1. As part of its 'Service Extraordinaire' initiative Novotel operates an in-hotel coaching system for staff training.

   CONSIDER: Whether such an in-house approach is likely to be better at keeping customer service standards high, rather than one using external training staff.

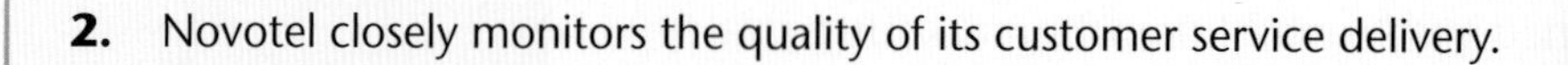

2. Novotel closely monitors the quality of its customer service delivery.

> **CONSIDER:** The views that staff and customers are likely to have about Novotel's methods of monitoring customer service quality.

3. Accor acquired twenty four UK hotels in 2007 and re-branded them as Mercure hotels. They have a similar target market to Novotel.

> **CONSIDER:** The extent of the challenge posed to Novotel by the introduction of Mecure hotels to the UK market place.

4. Novotel operates five Thalassa spa hotels in France and a range of Novotel Resort hotels with inclusive entertainment and activity packages around the world.

> **CONSIDER:** Whether these products within the Accor group could be successfully introduced in the UK.

5. In the UK, Novotel competes in a dynamic hotels market. The fastest-growing brand is the budget chain Travelodge.

> **CONSIDER:** The place of the Novotel brand in the ever-changing UK hotels market.

Discussion questions

(differentiated by level)

1. Review the staff training procedures that are in place in the Novotel brand's hotels in the UK (Level 3/GCE AS).
2. Assess the importance to Novotel's marketing strategy of below the line communications (Level 3/GCE AS).
3. Analyse the brand strengths of Novotel in relation to other members of the Accor Group (Foundation Degree).

11

The Giant's Causeway

– a natural attraction

Introduction

The Giant's Causeway is a natural visitor attraction on the coast of County Antrim in Northern Ireland. It is famous for its polygonal columns of igneous basalt rock, which are said to make it look like a road laid by a giant (see Figure 11.1). This part of the Giant's Causeway attraction is the Grand Causeway. Legend has it that the mythical Irish giant Finn MacCool built it to allow him to cross the sea to Scotland where similar rock formations are to be found on the island of Staffa in the Hebrides. The Giant's Causeway is the only World Heritage Site in Northern Ireland and is the focal point of a designated Area of Outstanding Natural Beauty (AONB). It is managed by the National Trust. The car

Figure 11.1 *– The Giant's Causeway (courtesy of Northern Ireland Tourist Board)*

park and tourist information centre on the cliff above are however, owned and operated by Moyle District Council. The Causeway is the centrepiece of a number of attractions along the Antrim Coast, including the Carrick-a-Rede rope bridge (see Figure 11.2) and Bushmills whiskey distillery.

Figure 11.2 *– Carrick-a-Rede rope bridge (courtesy of Northern Ireland Tourist Board)*

History and development

The Giant's Causeway is Northern Ireland's most famous tourist attraction. However, the Causeway itself is only part of the whole attraction. There are 6 km of spectacular sheer cliffs, rising to over 90 metres and forming a series of bays. The National Trust has provided a coastal path, which is about 8 km long, and leads from the entrance to the Causeway attraction. A small bus takes visitors who choose not to walk down the small cliff road to the Causeway itself.

In the Giant's Causeway complex as a whole there are about 37,000 polygonal rock columns. Most of them are hexagonal, but others have 4, 5, 7 or 8 sides. The columns were formed about 60 million years ago by the cooling and shrinking of molten rock. The tallest columns form a feature referred to as the Giant's Organ and are 12m high. As well as the Grand Causeway and the Giant's Organ, there are other formations with names including The Honeycomb and The Wishing Chair.

The Giant's Causeway has been a magnet for visitors to Northern Ireland since the mid-18th century. It was part of Cook's Tours itineraries a century ago. Europe's first hydro-electric tram ran between Portrush and the Giant's Causeway and was officially opened in 1883. For many tourists to the Antrim Coast in the late 19th and early 20th centuries, the tram journey along the picturesque coastline from the seaside resort of Portrush to the Giant's Causeway was a highlight of their annual holiday. The main tramline was closed in 1949 because of financial difficulties, but the link from Bushmills to the Causeway, which had opened in 1887, remained open another 2 years until 1951.

The Causeway's fame was increased by the recovery in 1967 and 1968 of the most valuable treasure found in a wrecked ship of the Spanish Armada, the sunken galleon the Girona. The treasure included 400 gold and 750 silver coins, gold jewellery, pendants, rings and cameos containing inset rubies and pearls, eight solid gold chains, plus silver forks and spoons. Although the most valuable items are in the Ulster Museum in Belfast, the story is told on picture boards at the Giant's Causeway.

The Causeway has developed considerably in scale as a managed attraction since the 1980s. The Giant's Causeway visitor centre opened in 1986, the same year that the attraction was designated a World Heritage Site. Apart from a tourist information centre, souvenir shops and a café-restaurant, the visitor centre houses an exhibition and audio-visual presentation explaining the geology of the Causeway and the legends associated with it. The separate and privately-owned Causeway Hotel is next to the Centre.

Structure

The total attraction of the Giant's Causeway is an assemblage of separately-owned and managed elements (see Figure 11.3):

- The shoreline and rock formations (the core natural attraction) are managed by the National Trust;
- The visitor centre and car park are owned and managed by Moyle District Council;
- The on-site bus service from the car park/ visitor centre complex to the stones is operated by Translink;
- The Causeway Hotel is a privately-run facility, next to the visitor centre.

In addition, the fact that the area has World Heritage Site status, and is in an area of Outstanding Natural Beauty, is an attraction in itself. World Heritage Sites are designated by UNESCO. The Giant's Causeway was chosen because it was judged to:

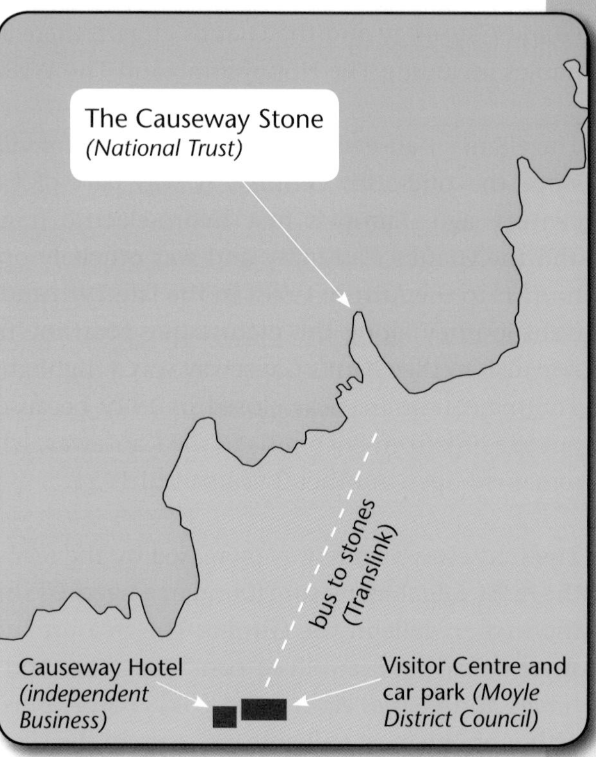

***Figure 11.3** – The Giant's Causeway attractions*

- Be a prime example of the Earth's geological history;
- Contain rare and superlative natural phenomena, as well as to have outstanding cultural value in the wrecked Spanish Armada ship, the Girona.

Operations

The attraction is open every day of the year except for Christmas and Boxing Days, although the shop and café are open for fewer hours than the car park. Admission is free, although donations to the National Trust, which is a voluntary sector organisation that is a registered charity, are welcome. Different opening arrangements apply to the visitor centre, the car park and the bus service down to the stones. The car park is charged and since it is operated by Moyle District Council, charges apply to all, including National Trust members. The visitor centre exhibition helps build the appeal of the attraction for school groups as well as families from the UK and further afield.

Staffing and customer service

The visitor centre staff team structure is shown in Figure 11.4. It is a hierarchical structure with the Centre Manager at its head. Below the other two management and supervisory level posts are six staff members working with customers at an operational level.

Visitor Centre Manager		
Assistant Manager		
Centre Supervisor		
3 Tourist Advisor/ Retail Assistants	2 Centre Attendants	1 Centre Attendant/ Retail Assistant

Figure 11.4 *– Visitor centre staffing hierarchy*

The Giant's Causeway is a natural attraction in a cliff scenery setting. Wild, ruggedness is part of its appeal to visitors. However, serving customers with mobility issues presents challenges to the organisations involved in the attraction's operation, as shown in Figure 11.5, which also lists some of the management solutions in place to address the issues.

Mobility challenges	Organisation	Management solutions
Accessing the stones at the bottom of cliffs, from the car park at the top	Translink	On-site bus service
Access to the facilities for disabled badge holders	Moyle District Council	Designated space close to facility buildings
Access to the visitor centre building and facilities	Moyle District Council	Ramped entrances to the visitor centre and shop, wheelchair and seating available. Accessible picnic tables
Toilet facilities	Moyle District Council	Adapted WC at the visitor centre
The nature of the site: uneven, narrow, loose gravel paths, steep slopes, many steps, varied and undulating terrain. The protrusion of sometimes slippery rock into the sea	National Trust	Map of accessible route made available

Figure 11.5 *– Mobility challenges at the Giant's Causeway*

Funding

The Giant's Causeway site, and 15 miles of footpaths along the 'Causeway Coastline', are owned and maintained by the National Trust. The National Trust is an independent, charitable organisation, which funds the conservation of important areas of the UK's natural landscape and of its built heritage. It manages the visitor attraction potential of its sites, financing its operations from money raised through donations, membership subscriptions, admission fees and sales, including its publications.

At the Giant's Causeway attraction, the National Trust works in partnership with Moyle District Council, which funds and manages the visitor centre and car park facilities, collecting revenue from café and shop sales and from car park fees.

Marketing

The Giant's Causeway is an 'iconic' UK attraction that has worldwide appeal in terms of its image and recognition. Photographs of the Causeway are used in tourist board promotional materials, including brochures, websites, exhibition displays and posters. The success of marketing the attraction can be judged in terms of the trend in visitor numbers. Figures 11.6 and 11.7 show yearly and monthly visitor statistics for the Giant's

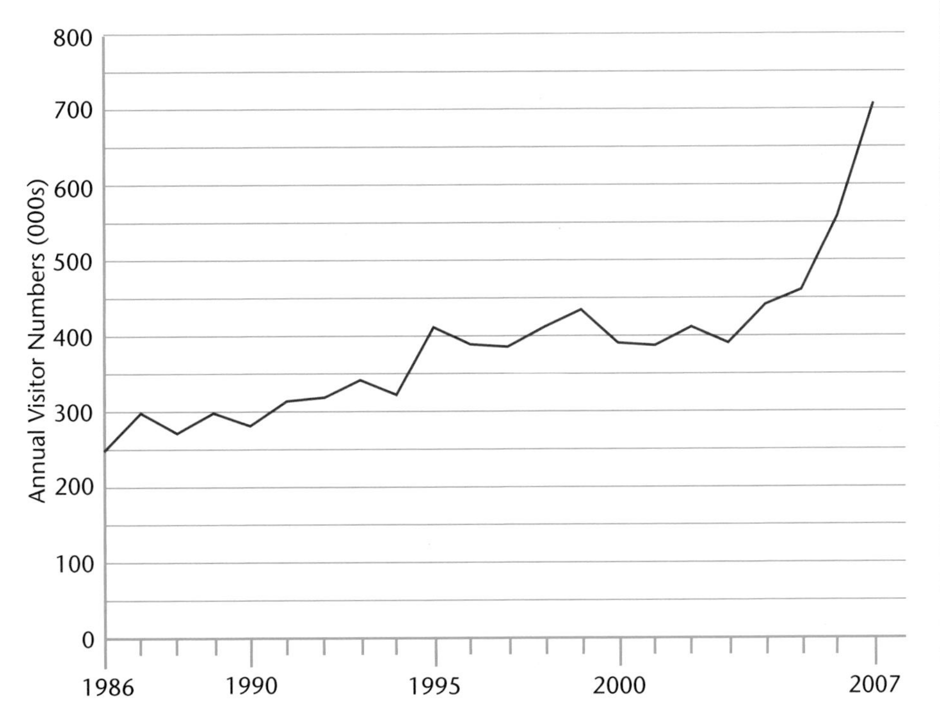

Figure 11.6 – Annual visitor numbers to the Giant's Causeway

Causeway visitor centre, based on car park data. It can be seen that visitors to the site have grown steadily since the 1986 visitor centre opening and World Heritage Site designation, from 250,000 in that year to more than 712,000 in 2007. Unsurprisingly, the monthly figures show a summer season peak from April to October, with August 2007 visitor numbers nearly nine times those of January, but visitor figures comfortably in excess of 10,000 in every month.

Month	Visitor numbers
January	15,455
February	20,548
March	30,625
April	75,216
May	67,221
June	73,617
July	110,447
August	138,463
September	79,595
October	55,459
November	26,589
December	19,479

***Figure 11.7** – Monthly 2007 visitor numbers to the Giant's Causeway*

Future

Extrapolation of the visitor number statistics for the Giant's Causeway shown in Figure 11.6 suggests that the recent accelerating expansion is set to continue into the foreseeable future. Consideration will need to be given to the future capacity of the current facilities at the site, including the visitor centre and car park.

In 2007 the Northern Ireland Executive announced its intention to have the private sector build a new visitor centre. However, this proposal met immediate opposition from the National Trust, which said it could call into question the Giant's Causeway's continued status as a World Heritage Site. The Trust's Northern Ireland Director expressed her concern that such a new centre would "set a disastrous precedent for development, so close to the World Heritage Site".

Issues to consider

1. The Giant's Causeway is a 'honeypot' attraction.

CONSIDER: Possible strategies for managing the Giant's Causeway sustainably as a visitor attraction.

2. The management of different aspects of the Giant's Causeway site is divided between different organisations.

CONSIDER: The potential impacts of this on the quality of the visitor experience.

3. A new visitor centre for the area was proposed in 2007.

CONSIDER: The pros and cons of such a development.

4. The Giant's Causeway is one of several attractions along the Antrim Coast.

CONSIDER: The place of the Giant's Causeway in the tourism development of Antrim and the opportunities and threats arising from having such a cluster of attractions in a coastal location.

5. The Giant's Causeway is a World Heritage Site (WHS).

CONSIDER: (a) the benefits this designation gives to the conservation of the Causeway; (b) the implications of WHS status on the future development of the Causeway as a visitor attraction.

6. As an iconic attraction, the Giant's Causeway is an element in many tour operators' Northern Ireland itineraries.

CONSIDER: The network of travel and tourism organisations whose businesses benefit from the appeal of the Giant's Causeway as a visitor attraction.

Discussion questions

(differentiated by level)

1. The Giant's Causeway is a natural attraction in Northern Ireland. Analyse the range of visitor attraction types in one region you have studied or know about (Level 3/GCE AS).

2. The Giant's Causeway is a 'must-see' attraction for many visitors to Ireland. It has World Heritage Site status.

   (a) Describe the range of tourism impacts the Causeway experiences;

   (b) Assess the extent to which you think WHS designation helps in the management of these impacts (Level 3/GCE A2).

3. In 2007, a new, private sector visitor centre was proposed for the Giant's Causeway. Discuss the apparent fragmentation of management of the Giant's Causeway World Heritage Site and propose an outline strategy for a co-ordinated approach in the future (Foundation Degree).

Durham Cathedral

– a heritage attraction

Introduction

Durham Cathedral (see Figure 12.1) is a historic cathedral in Durham City. It was built in the late 11th and early 12th centuries, though its tallest tower was added later, and is impressively sited on a prominent, elevated site in a meander of the River Wear. As well as being an active Christian church, Durham Cathedral, together with the neighbouring Durham Castle (pictured right in Figure 12.1) is a World Heritage Site. It is a major heritage tourism attraction in North East England. Over 600,000 people from all over the world visit the Cathedral annually. The Cathedral contains the shrine

Figure 12.1 – Durham Cathedral and Castle

of St Cuthbert and the tomb of St Bede. It is widely considered to be the finest example of Norman architecture in England.

History and development

Because it houses the shrine of St Cuthbert, Durham Cathedral has a history as a place of pilgrimage that stretches back to the time of its construction. Pilgrims are religious tourists and so the Cathedral's history as a tourist attraction is equally long. After the Middle Ages, the Cathedral became a place that also appealed to secular tourists because of its status as a major historical monument. Through the 19th and 20th centuries its popularity as a visitor attraction grew.

Durham Cathedral (and Castle) was listed as a World Heritage Site (WHS) in 1986, the same year as the Giant's Causeway (see Case Study 11), Stonehenge, Avebury prehistoric stone circle and the Tower of London. WHSs are listed by UNESCO (the United Nations Educational Scientific and Cultural Organisation) because they are seen as places that are so special that it is the duty of the whole international community to conserve them for future generations. In the case of Durham Cathedral, it was the building's architectural significance and its important place in Christian history, as the home of the relics of St Cuthbert and St Bede, that led to its designation as a WHS.

Structure and Operations

The Cathedral is managed by the Durham Cathedral Chapter, a church body established for the purpose under the auspices of the Dean – a senior member of the diocesan clergy who is responsible to the Bishop.

Because it is a church, and therefore a place of worship, admission to Durham Cathedral is free. However, tourist visitors are encouraged to make a donation of a few pounds towards the upkeep of the fabric of the building. In principle, the Cathedral is open to visitors every day, but, in practice, access is restricted during religious services and when ceremonial events are being held in the building. Sunday opening hours are restricted to the afternoon to allow time for morning and evening religious services.

Inside the Cathedral, the Chapter levies charges for admission to the internal attractions:

- The Treasures of St Cuthbert exhibition;
- The Monk's Dormitory – one of the remaining vestiges of the Cathedral's medieval function as a monastery;
- The tallest of Durham Cathedral's three towers – whose roof is opened to visitors so that they can enjoy views across the city, the river and the surrounding wooded countryside.

Next to the Treasury, the Cathedral Café provides an additional revenue stream for the Chapter.

The principal free attractions inside are the nave itself, completed in 1128 and using, for the time, revolutionary building techniques, the Shrine of St Cuthbert and the tomb of the Venerable Bede in the internal Galilee Chapel. Volunteers and clergy act as tourist guides and monitor behaviour, intervening discretely when the latter is deemed inappropriate for a house of God. Guided tours are provided in summer – up to 4 a day in the peak season months of August and September.

As well as individual visitors, Durham Cathedral attracts many education groups. In response to the demand from schools, the Cathedral Chapter operates its own Education Service. This provides activities and resources to support teachers of Religious Education and help with the delivery of broader aspects of the National Curriculum, including the secondary school subjects of history and art.

Staffing and customer service

Durham Cathedral Chapter manage the building both as a place of religious worship (their main priority) and as a secular visitor attraction. The Dean heads the Chapter.

Managing visitors is not only part and parcel of opening the building to tourists, it is also important to direct them away from places and times in the Cathedral and its life where they may, usually unwittingly, negatively impact on the building's primary, religious function. This visitor management requires a team of experienced members of staff. However, staffing costs have to be kept as low as possible because the Cathedral relies entirely on voluntary contributions for its income, apart from the proceeds of what are seen as their secondary visitor attraction facilities. Savings are made by using voluntary rather than paid staff whenever possible, for example to provide information and guiding services, and to staff the internal attractions themselves. An additional personnel requirement is the staffing of the Cathedral Café.

As well as the lay volunteers, members of the Cathedral clergy act as impromptu tourist information providers and keep an eye on customer behaviour. They will speak quietly to any member of the visiting public whose conduct is seen as inappropriate or disrespectful in a religious place.

The Cathedral's Education Service is staffed by a salaried Education Officer and Education Assistant and by a team of volunteers. In line with the legal requirements governing adults working with children, all the education team have Criminal Records' Bureau (CRB) clearance. It is always the case that children and students taking part in educational visits and, as a spin-off, their families, are important to visitor attractions as potential future customers. In the case of Durham Cathedral, the managing Chapter see this as secondary and prefer that they return to the Cathedral in its role as a church.

Finance and funding

The total cost of running the Cathedral as an active church, education centre and visitor attraction is around £3 million per year. The Cathedral Chapter is the management body responsible for all aspects of the Cathedral's operations. The Chapter does not receive any money from the UK government for maintaining and operating the Cathedral, unlike national museums for instance, but instead relies on collections from worshippers and donations made by supporters and visitors. The savings made by using voluntary rather than paid staff as guides and information providers contribute to managing the finances by helping reduce costs. So, although admission to the majority of the building is free, visitors are invited to make a significant donation towards the running costs of the Cathedral. Research has shown that the income in 2007 amounted to approximately £4 per adult visitor. British tax payers are also invited to use Gift Aid envelopes which are made available, so that the Chapter can reclaim the tax payable for any donations received.

Marketing

Given that the primary purpose of Durham Cathedral remains religious, marketing as a tourist attraction is relatively restrained. Nevertheless, it does take place. An increasingly important promotional tool for the Chapter of Durham Cathedral is their website. Not least among its marketing aims is the communication of the religious sanctity of the site. However, there is also some attempt to sell visits to the Cathedral. The Education Service, for example, promotes:

- The 'hands-on' nature of the teaching and learning activities provided;
- Durham Cathedral as a unique educational resource which 'cannot be replicated in the classroom', so promoting the idea that an actual trip is essential;
- The range of activities and resources available;
- The adaptability of the Education Service staff to meet schools' needs.

The use of e-marketing is exemplified by the website's changing list of currently available educational activities and by a dedicated education service e-mailbox to allow online negotiation of tailor-made visits.

Future

Durham Cathedral is part of the Durham Cathedral and Castle World Heritage Site. Being a WHS means that there is a management plan drawn up to chart its intended future development, and to map out how this can be done in a sustainable manner. As a complete entity, the WHS is managed by its three owners – the Cathedral Chapter, Durham University and St John's College, which co-operated with other stakeholder members of the WHS Management Plan Steering Group, including Durham City

Council and English Heritage, when compiling the plan. Their aims for the management of the Durham WHS include:

- Maintaining 'the quality and distinctiveness of the World Heritage Site's environment' – keeping it as good as it is now into the future;
- Allowing the site's varied religious, educational and visitor attraction uses to continue, with minimal negative impact on each other;
- Carefully controlling the land use of the WHS to allow for its sustainable development, including as a visitor attraction;
- Realising more fully the educational potential of the site.

The WHS Management Plan sets out a future vision of the Durham Peninsula (see Figure 12.2), on which the Cathedral and Durham Castle stand, as:

"a holy and tranquil place that is inspiring and life enhancing for all who come into contact with it . . . a welcoming and atmospheric space with a strong sense of its own identity, providing sanctuary from the pressures of everyday life".

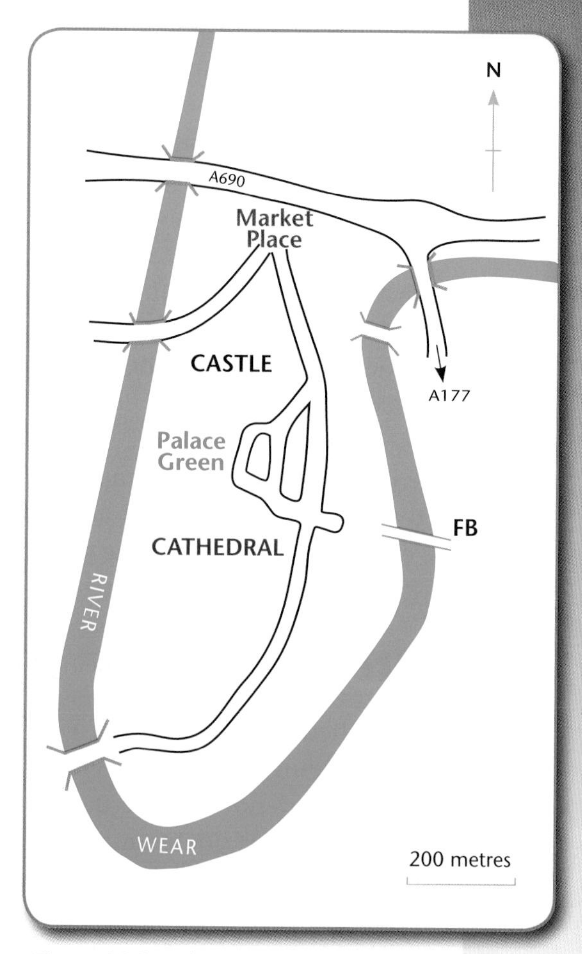

***Figure 12.2** – The Durham Peninsula*

This is not the language of 'mass tourism'. A key challenge for the future management of the Durham World Heritage Site is to meet the aim of developing the visitor attraction function in such a way as to not impact negatively on the environmental qualities quoted above. The Durham Cathedral and Castle WHS Management Plan will be reviewed and revised in 2011.

Issues to consider

1. Durham Cathedral is primarily a religious building, but it is also a major visitor attraction.

CONSIDER: The extent to which the Cathedral's development as a tourist attraction is in conflict with the building's primary purpose.

2. Durham Cathedral is part of a World Heritage Site (WHS).

CONSIDER: The advantages of WHS designation for a heritage attraction such as Durham Cathedral.

3. The Durham Cathedral and Castle WHS was one of the first to be designated in the UK, in 1986. Best practice management procedures and structures found at most other UK World Heritage Sites were not put in place in Durham until after its Management Plan was published in 2006.

CONSIDER: How a WHS designated later than 1986 is likely to be better placed to manage its development sustainably.

4. Durham Castle shares the World Heritage Site designation with the Cathedral. The Norman Castle is used as university student accommodation as well as being a visitor attraction in its own right. It has been in such poor condition as a building that it has been included on English Heritage's 'Buildings at Risk' Register.

CONSIDER: The possible impacts of Durham Castle on the development of the Cathedral as a visitor attraction.

5. When the Durham World Heritage Site was designated by UNESCO, its boundary was drawn tightly around the two main buildings. This meant that areas such as the medieval square of Palace Green, which separates them, was not included. Palace Green, the historic streets and wooded river banks that surround the originally-designated WHS are important in creating its atmosphere.

CONSIDER: The implications of extending the WHS to include the areas surrounding the Cathedral and Castle.

6. Durham Cathedral is sited at the top of a hill with only one narrow, medieval street connecting it to the Market Place in the modern city centre. The Durham Cathedral Bus has been provided as a sustainable transport service to improve accessibility.

CONSIDER: The extent to which heritage attractions such as Durham Cathedral can genuinely provide access for all potential customers.

Discussion questions

(differentiated by level)

1. What are the essential differences between heritage, natural and built visitor attractions? Use examples to illustrate your answer (Level3/GCE AS).

2. Discuss the issues that arise from managing a major heritage building as a visitor attraction (Level 3/GCE A2).

3. Durham Cathedral and Castle was one of the first World Heritage Sites listed in the UK. Assess the extent to which this has been a blessing and a curse for the Cathedral's management (Foundation Degree).

13

Legoland Windsor

– a built attraction

Introduction

Legoland Windsor is a theme park situated to the west of London. It was built to be a tourist attraction, in contrast to Durham Cathedral for example (see Case Study 12), which, like many heritage attractions, was built for another purpose and became a tourist attraction at a later date.

***Figure 13.1** – The entrance to Legoland Windsor*

The theme for Legoland Windsor theme park is the Lego construction toy. The toy is Danish in origin and the first Legoland theme park was in Denmark. The name Legoland Windsor distinguishes the UK theme park from the Danish original and from the two other Legolands in Germany and the USA. Windsor, largely due to its castle being an important royal residence, is a historic tourism destination in itself.

History and development

Ole Kirk Christiansen founded the Lego toy company in Denmark in 1934. The name comes from the Danish words 'leg godt', meaning 'play well'. The first Legoland theme park was opened in Billund in Denmark in 1968. Legoland Windsor began operating in 1996 on the site of what had been Windsor Safari Park, a tourist attraction that went into receivership in 1992. After acquiring the site, Lego spent 4 years and used 25 million Lego bricks to develop the park with the Lego theme. Two more Legoland theme parks have opened more recently – Legoland California in 1999 and Legoland Deutschland (Germany) in 2002. In 2005 ownership of Legoland Windsor, and the other three theme parks, changed as the Lego company and Merlin Entertainments came together to run the parks, with Lego keeping a 30% share.

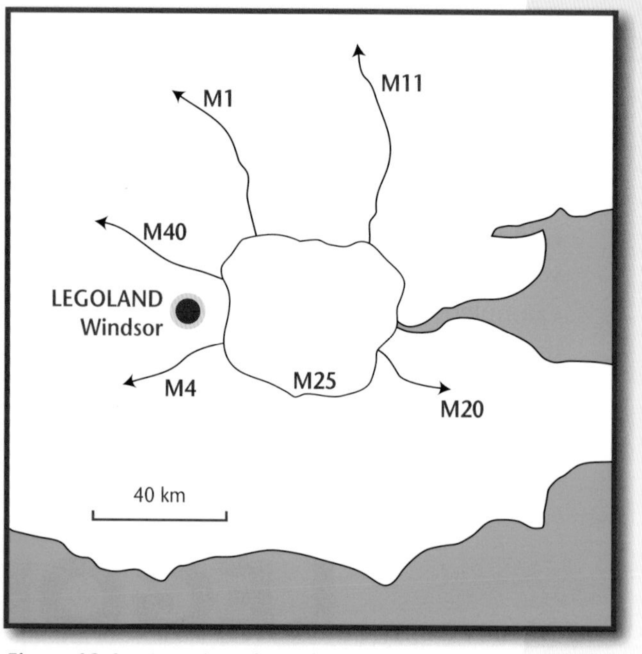

Figure 13.2 – Location of Legoland Windsor

In 2007, the first Legoland Discovery Centre (indoor, interactive attractions to be located in city centres) opened in Berlin. In addition, Legoland Atlantis by Sea Life, another brand owned by Merlin Entertainments, opened in Billund, Denmark.

Ownership structure

Since 2005 the four Legoland theme parks have been part of the Merlin Entertainments Group. This is, in turn, backed by Blackstone Venture Capital, an American private equity investment firm. The Lego Group itself retains a 30% share of the Legoland theme parks' business.

Attraction type	UK	Rest of Europe
Theme parks	**Alton Towers** – theme park in Staffordshire. Apart from rides it has two themed hotels, indoor and outdoor water parks, spa and conference centre.	**Gardaland** – Italy's largest theme park with over 40 rides and the Gardaland Resort Hotel.
	Thorpe Park – theme park in Surrey with over 25 rides and attractions.	**Heide Park** – theme park in Germany, home to the world's tallest drop tower, Scream, a 440-bed holiday centre and resort hotel.
	Chessington World of Adventures – rides, zoo animals, live shows and hotel.	
Themed attractions	**Sea Life** – 11 of the 23 Sea Life aquaria and 3 marine sanctuaries are in the UK.	**Earth Explorer, Belgium** – an interactive attraction about planet Earth
	British Airways London Eye – the world's tallest observation wheel.	
	Madame Tussauds – waxworks in London for over 200 years. Also, New York, Amsterdam, Las Vegas, Shanghai, Hong Kong and soon Washington DC and Hollywood.	
	Dungeons – live actors, rides, shows and special effects in dark, dungeon-like environments in London, Edinburgh, York, Hamburg and Amsterdam.	
	Warwick Castle – marketed as a medieval experience with themed attractions and entertainment.	

Figure 13.3 *– Merlin Entertainments' visitor attractions*

Merlin Entertainments Group is Europe's largest visitor attractions operator, and second largest in the world after Disney. Merlin operates 50 visitor attractions in 12 different countries worldwide, including brands such as Sea Life, the Dungeons (the London and Edinburgh Dungeons, for example), Madame Tussauds and the British Airways London Eye. Altogether, Merlin attractions welcomed around 30 million visitors in 2006 and employed approximately 13,000 people at peak times. Figure 13.3 summarises the structure of Merlin's visitor attractions portfolio in the UK and Europe, other than the four Legolands.

Operations

Legoland Windsor operates over 50 rides and interactive attractions, as well as eleven restaurants and cafés, plus seven shops. A typical customer's visit lasts between 5 and 6 hours, so the shops and catering outlets are useful opportunities for the operators to increase revenue above ticket income – this is known as 'secondary spend'.

Products and service operations can be grouped as follows:

- Rides and attractions;
- Events and shows;
- Catering;
- Education.

Rides include the Dragon Coaster (see Figure 13.4), Pirate Falls water chute and the Lego Driving School, where children can drive small electric cars. Miniland is an attraction made up of large-scale Lego models of monuments and famous buildings in Europe, including London's Big Ben and Tower Bridge. The Lego Creation Centre features Lego set pieces including the Wall of Fame's Lego brick portraits of famous people.

An events calendar is published on the Legoland website www.legoland.co.uk, featuring spectaculars that change with the seasons. In 2007, for example, Halloween was marked by a 'witches and wizards fireworks spectacular' on the Saturday night of 3 November. Shows include fairytale plays for younger children at the Duplo Theatre and live-action spectaculars, such as 'Johnny Thunder and the Revenge of Aztec Queen'.

Figure 13.4 – The Dragon Coaster ride at Legoland Windsor

Shops include souvenir outlets, the sale of photographs taken on rides and fashion wear. Catering outlets include carts and kiosks, the Jungle Café and Knights Table Rotisserie restaurant, offering meals for breakfast and lunch time and snacks, sweets and ice creams all day.

Legoland Active Learning Programmes are provided in the Discovery Zone workshops and at Robolab, where computer-controlled Lego robots are built by children during educational workshop sessions.

Staffing

At peak times, Legoland Windsor employs up to 155 full-time staff and a further 775 seasonal staff. The summer season itself is obviously very busy, but so are other periods such as the October half-term holiday.

Two operational level job roles that are particular to Legoland Windsor are model maker and landscaper.

Model makers

A team of six full-time model makers build the Lego models that create the Lego theme for Legoland Windsor theme park. There are now over 50 million bricks in use at the park. The Lego models are first designed by hand on graph paper. For larger models, a prototype is built. When models of buildings are to be made, model makers visit the site of the subject building to photograph it first. When the Lego brick models are completed they are glued together to ensure they are sufficiently robust. The Miniland models, for example, stand outside all year round, so have to be able to withstand all types of weather. As well as making new Lego models for the park, the six model makers also clean and maintain existing models.

Landscapers

The grounds of Legoland Windsor occupy over 60 hectares. The inner park – the part actually accessible to visitors – amounts to 29 acres in total. The landscaping of the basin-like site is regarded as making an important contribution to the quality of the visitors' experience of the park. That, in turn, is significant in terms of repeat business and recommendations that actual customers make to potential customers. Legoland Windsor's own market research shows that over 97% of visitors rate the landscape of the park as 'very good'.

Legoland Windsor has been developed on the former site of Windsor Safari Park and is bordered by Windsor Great Park. It is a naturally scenic area with historic oak trees, some of which are up to 300 years old. It is something of a horticultural challenge for landscapers to successfully blend this inherited planting with the exotic plants used to help create a theme park ambience, for example using palm trees. In Miniland, great care has to be taken to work around the Lego models of European buildings that have been located there. The team of landscapers has to bear in mind that target market visitors are children whose view of the models they have come to see can easily be disrupted by planting that an adult would be likely to see over easily.

Funding and finance

Legoland Windsor is one of Merlin Entertainments Group UK visitor attractions. Capital for the on-going development of the park, for projects such as the Viking land area that was new for 2007, comes from investment. Merlin Entertainments is, in turn, substantially funded by the private equity provider Blackstone Venture Capital, an American investment firm which in 2007 also bid to take over the Hilton Hotels chain. The Lego corporation itself is a 30% shareholder in Legoland theme parks, including the UK operation at Windsor. Another source of funding for individual rides and attractions is the set of partner businesses with which Legoland has entered into arrangements. Turnover comes from the revenue that customer visits generate. Aside from ticket sales, revenue streams include the profits earned from the 11 on-site catering outlets.

Marketing

The target market for Legoland Windsor is well-defined – families with children from 3 to 12 years old. The choice of location for the theme park (see Figure 13.2) was heavily influenced by the fact that 9 million families with young children live within a two-hour drive of the attraction. Further locational advantage arises from the theme park's proximity to both Windsor and London. Tourist families visiting either destination may be attracted to spend a day at Legoland. In addition, Legoland's own visitors may feel it appropriate to visit the tourist town because of their theme park trip.

Legoland Windsor has a very well-defined theme – the Lego construction toy. The themes of other theme parks in the UK are sometimes less well-defined, either by the name (Alton Towers, for example) or by adherence to the theme (Camelot). While some theme parks in France (Disneyland Paris and Parc Asterix for instance) are clearly themed, it is interesting to note that the French for 'theme park' is 'parc d'attractions' (attractions park), which perhaps better describes the function of the UK's so-called 'theme parks'.

Legoland Windsor's clear theme is helpful in marketing the attraction to visitors, since the target market has a clear perception of the offer that is made to them. However, it also makes the issue of repeat business more challenging. This is because of a 'checklist effect'. Parents may feel that they have satisfied one demand of their children by visiting Legoland and so they can tick that off their list. To try to conteract this effect, Legoland Windsor offers annual passes to attract people to visit more than once. In 2006 over 50,000 of these were taken up by customers. Certainly, market research findings indicate that there is a sizeable potential market for repeat visits – 90% of customers in 2006 thought that their visit to the park had been 'good' or 'excellent'. The attraction also has a series of events that change regularly, so that visitors have another reason to visit the park for a second time.

Future

Since 2005, Legoland Windsor has been owned by Merlin Entertainments. New developments since then have marked a change of direction – a move away from the purely out-of-town Lego-themed parks to a more diversified product. In 2007, the first interactive, city-centre Legoland Discovery Centre began operating in Berlin, as did the twin-themed Legoland Atlantis by Sea Life attraction in Denmark. If these ventures prove successful, Merlin may choose to make similar investments elsewhere. Growing markets in the Far East, such as China, are one clear possibility.

Issues to consider

1. Legoland Windsor has a clear target market – families with young children.

CONSIDER: The advantages and disadvantages for Legoland Windsor of appealing to one specific market segment.

2. Lego is a traditional construction toy.

CONSIDER: How well Legoland Windsor is adapting to the technological developments that are happening in children's lives.

3. Legoland Windsor has a clear theme. The themes of other UK theme parks are often less well-defined.

CONSIDER: The extent to which theme parks in the UK are actually themed.

4. Merlin Entertainments are diversifying the Legoland product.

CONSIDER: Why this may be an appropriate future strategy for Legoland's owners to pursue.

5. While 90% of Legoland Windsor's 2006 customers enjoyed their visit to the theme park, fewer (65%) thought that the price they had paid represented good value for money.

CONSIDER: The implications of these figures for marketing Legoland Windsor.

Discussion questions

(differentiated by level)

1. (a) Evaluate the extent to which Legoland Windsor's facilities are consistent with the park's theme (Level 3/GCE AS).

(b) Analyse the themed facilities available at other UK theme parks (Level 3/GCE AS).

2. A family visiting the UK from overseas and including two children in Legoland's target market age range plan to stay in the Windsor area for three days. Draft an itinerary for their visit, including a day spent at Legoland Windsor (Level 3/GCE A2).

3. Legoland Windsor is one of four Legoland parks in the world. The original is in Denmark and there are two further parks in Germany and the USA. Outline the issues for Merlin Entertainments in considering the feasibility of opening a Lego-themed attraction in a country in Asia (Foundation Degree).

14

South West Tourism

– a Regional Tourist Board

Introduction

South West Tourism is the Regional Tourist Board (RTB) for the South West of England. Its role is to work with and encourage other travel and tourism organisations to promote and develop tourism in South West England – Bath, Bristol, Bournemouth/Poole, Cornwall and the Isles of Scilly, Devon, Dorset, Somerset, Gloucestershire (including Cotswolds and Forest of Dean destinations) and Wiltshire, as shown in Figure 14.1. South West Tourism (SWT) is a partnership of organisations from the private, public and voluntary sectors of the tourist economy.

There are nine Regional Tourist Boards (RTBs) in England:

- South West Tourism
- Tourism South East
- VisitLondon
- East of England Tourist Board
- Heart of England Tourist Board
- One North East
- East Midlands Tourism
- Yorkshire Tourist Board
- North West of England Tourist Board

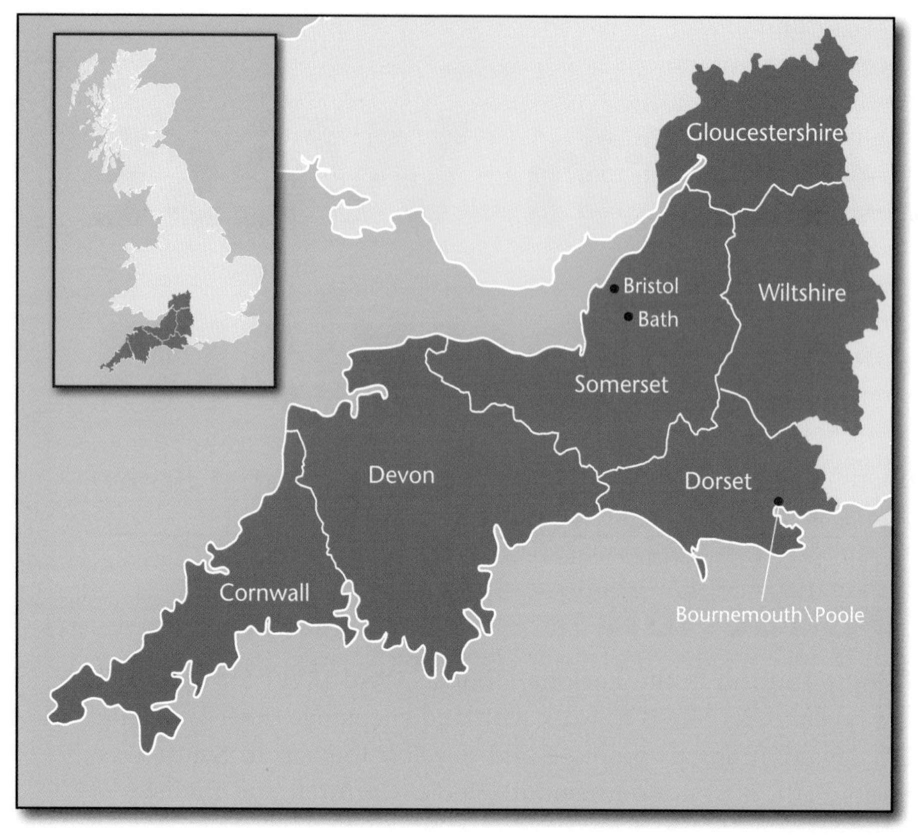

***Figure 14.1** – South West Tourism's region*

In recent years, South West England has been the destination of around 20% of all the tourist trips made in England. In 2006, just over 20 million trips were made to the South West by UK residents alone, as the figures from the UK Tourism Survey shown in Figure 14.2 indicate.

Visitor spending in the South West has brought over £5 billion into the economy of the region, creating about a quarter of a million jobs. Direct, indirect and induced impacts affect more or less every town and village in the South West, supporting jobs, local businesses and local infrastructure. More than 10,000 travel and tourism organisations provide the region's visitor attractions and tourist accommodation. They are of all scales but include many SMEs (small and medium-sized enterprises) and family businesses such as rural bed and breakfast establishments, country inns and hotels, in addition to providers of adventure sports activities such as surfing, sailing and mountain biking. Many additional businesses belonging to other industries such as retailing and catering, as well as transport providers, rely on tourism income for their survival.

Region visited	No. of trips (millions) 2006
West Midlands	8.36
East of England	10.69
East Midlands	8.36
London	10.96
North West	13.53
North East	3.43
South East	18.14
South West	20.31
Yorkshire and Humberside	10.07

***Figure 14.2** – Trips to English regions in 2006*

Development

South West Tourism (or the South West Tourist Board) has promoted travel and tourism and represented the interests of travel and tourism businesses in the region for over 30 years. The organisation has developed to the extent that it now has more than 5,000 member organisations, including hotels, tourist attractions, transport operators, local authority tourism departments and voluntary organisations.

Structure and staffing

South West Tourism currently has 45 staff, with a senior management team of six people led by the Chief Executive. The South West Tourism Board is made up of 15 Directors (of whom three are Executive Directors). The Chair is one of the remaining twelve Non-Executive Directors.

The Board aims to represent the interests of the regional travel and tourism industry, including South West Tourism's 5,000 members, and those of the wider local community. With two exceptions, Non-Executive Directors are appointed to join the Board. They are selected by the other Directors after an open recruitment process. Visit Britain's CEO and the South West Regional Development Agency's Chief Executive are ex-officio members of the Board. New appointments to the Board are subject to confirmation at the organisation's Annual General Meeting.

Operations and customer service

South West Tourism's raison d'etre is to promote and support tourism to and within the South West of England. It operates its services to achieve this aim. Its customers are travel and tourism providers, particularly its members, and the region's tourists.

For example, South West Tourism provides its 5,000 member organisations with business support services, including weekly email updates on industry developments, providing marketing opportunities through inter-member networking and negotiated savings with some infrastructure and support service organisations. South West Tourism also operates the Visit South West website www.visitsouthwest.co.uk. Here, members can advertise their businesses for half the price that South West Tourism charges non-members. It maintains a Business Services Directory so that members can access additional services to help their regional tourism businesses, including consultancy, print suppliers, designers and photography specialists. These support services are aimed at helping SMEs in particular. As the principal regional voice on tourism, South West Tourism also represents its members' interests nationally, contributing, for example, to government tourism policy discussions on their behalf.

Customer perceptions of service quality are very important in promoting tourism anywhere, whether in the UK or overseas. South West Tourism operates in partnership with The Tourism Skills Network South West to provide training courses for the tourism industry, including 'Welcome to Excellence' customer service courses. These courses include Welcome Host and Welcome Host Plus, Welcome All and Welcome Management as well as 'Green Awareness' sustainable tourism training.

South West Tourism helps destinations in the region to set up Destination Management Organisations (DMOs), whose aim is to gain best value for public money spent on tourism by helping to develop partnerships between tourism organisations from the public, private and voluntary sectors. The idea is that tourism is more likely to grow where close partnerships exist between regional and local agents of development. By 2007, the following nine South West England destinations had been identified for DMO set up:

1. Bath;
2. Bournemouth & Poole;
3. Bristol;
4. Cornwall;
5. Devon;
6. Dorset;
7. Gloucestershire (Cotswolds and Forest of Dean);
8. Somerset;
9. Wiltshire.

These destinations were selected after research showed that they were the most visitor-recognised destinations in the South West, with the necessary size, scale and capacity to deliver results.

South West Tourism (SWT) provides travel and tourism businesses with information to help them keep up to date with tourism issues. Members have access to South West Tourism's bank of consumer research data to help them plan and develop their businesses more successfully. SMEs can take advantage of networking opportunities provided by South West Tourism to harness consultancy services so that they exploit this database for maximum benefit. SWT operates a research department which can provide tailor-made, though charged, research services as members require them. Target customer profiling is a system developed by the English Regional Tourist Boards collectively and supplied by SWT for travel and tourism businesses in the region to use to profile existing and likely potential new customers.

SWT is also involved in the dissemination of information to the region's tourist visitors. It researches the needs of the region's tourists and looks for different ways to meet them better. The Board's market research shows that tourists rate access to information while they are on holiday as one of the most important factors in their enjoyment. Many visitors to the South West are touring or self-packaging, often from different regions of the UK, and make substantial use of information services. Gleaning information from Tourist Information Centres (TICs) is one of the most popular means, although accommodation providers, leaflets, texts and information boards are also important sources.

Tourist Information Centres are independent bodies. They are funded and managed by partnerships including local authorities, tourist associations, museums and private individuals. They also receive support from VisitBritain. South West Tourism acts as a co-ordinating agency to facilitate the work of these disparate partners in providing tourist information services throughout the region.

In 2006, South West Tourism produced 'tourism information guidelines' to help providers supply information services that were clearly focused on customers' needs. From 2007, tourism information 'official partners' are being introduced. These are organisations and individuals that provide tourists with information. Premises display signs notifying tourists that these providers have 'official partner' status. To earn the right to do so, providers have to meet a range of quality, sustainability, training and customer service criteria. Customers can be confident about the accuracy of information and quality of service they will receive from such partners, whose own businesses benefit from resulting spin-off trade.

Government funding

Since 2003, responsibility for tourism in the English regions has been devolved to the Regional Development Agencies (RDAs). The South West RDA Chief Executive, and the CEO of VisitBritain, sit on the South West Tourism Board. The South West Regional Development Agency (SWRDA) is one of nine RDAs in England. Their main focus is the economic development, including tourism development, of their regions. Together, they have a government-funded budget of £2 billion per annum and are responsible for implementing Regional Sustainable Tourism Strategies, in line with government policy. The SWRDA is a key player in the leadership of tourism development in the South West and works with a range of regional and local partners, including South West Tourism.

VisitBritain is the main public sector organisation involved in promoting the UK as a whole as a tourism destination. It receives money from the Government to market the UK and England as tourist destinations. In 2003-2004, for example, funding from the Department for Culture, Media and Sport (DCMS) was £35.5m for promoting Britain overseas as a tourist destination, and £14.1m for marketing tourism to England within the UK.

VisitBritain champions the tourism, creative and leisure industries in the UK and is responsible for government policy in these areas, including domestic tourism in England and incoming tourism to Britain. The VisitEngland home page on the internet is part of VisitBritain's marketing of England as a tourist destination. Scotland, Wales and Northern Ireland have devolved governments and so tourism policies are developed locally, but in co-operation with the DCMS.

Marketing

Regional Tourist Boards like South West Tourism play a leading part in marketing their regions as tourism destinations. SWT and the South West Regional Development Agency together promote travel and tourism to the region. The aims of their marketing strategy are to:

- Promote the South West as a destination that offers varied, high quality and value-for-money holidays all year round;
- Support responsible tourism and sustainable development;
- Encourage repeat visits;
- Establish clearly the area that is defined as the South West;
- Represent the regional environment balances of coast and countryside, and city and rural places.

South West Tourism has discovered from market research that visitors make holiday choices that are based on the experiences they want to have when they visit a destination. From their research, SWT have identified eight experiences to promote. Each experience has been branded and given its own dedicated web site, targeted at a definite market segment and supported by a marketing campaign (see Figure 14.3).

SWT's marketing department produces a variety of promotional material. The principal aims of the department are to:

- Run marketing campaigns;
- Keep the South West region and its tourism industry in the media spotlight;
- Keep SWT's members informed.

Experience brand	Website	Target market segment
Sheer Indulgence	**www.indulgesouthwest.co.uk**	Wealthy couples and customers celebrating a special occasion
Close to Nature	**www.naturesouthwest.co.uk**	Customers with a particular interest in the countryside and the outdoors
It's Adventure!	**www.itsadventuresouthwest.co.uk**	Singles, couples and groups looking for exciting, physical activity
Family Holidays - Beach & Beyond!	**www.familyholidaysouthwest.co.uk**	Families with children
Easy Preschool	**www.easypreschoolsouthwest.co.uk**	Families with children aged under 5
History & Heritage	**www.livingheritagesouthwest.co.uk**	Customers seeking cultural and historical experiences
Relax and Recharge	**www.relaxsouthwest.co.uk**	Family and friendship groups who want to spend some quality time together
Romantic Escapes	**www.romancesouthwest.co.uk**	Couples planning a romantic break or wedding

Figure 14.3 *– South West Tourism brands*

The marketing department sends SWT members weekly email updates with tourism news, details of membership benefits, political issues affecting tourism, research data and security advice. It also helps members promote their businesses online and monitors visitor numbers, so that it can plan campaigns designed to benefit SWT members as much as possible.

SWT's press office liaises with newspaper and magazine editors in the region and nationally, issuing press releases to try to keep potential visitors' awareness of the South West of England high. Another purpose of high-profile media coverage is so that business, politicians and local people in general are educated about tourism's economic importance to the region. An example of a SWT press release is shown in Figure 14.4.

OVER 300 TOURISM PIONEERS!

South West Tourism is pleased to announce that over 300 tourism 'pioneer' businesses in the South West have now joined the Green Tourism Business Scheme (GTBS) - more than any other English region.

The scheme rewards businesses for their green actions, including reducing energy, water, waste and support of the local economy . . .

***Figure 14.4** – Extract from a South West Tourism press release*

Future

South West Tourism and the South West Regional Development Agency have jointly developed a ten-year strategic plan for tourism in the region, called Towards 2015 - Shaping Tomorrow's Tourism. Its three main aims are to:

- Develop tourism sustainably;
- Raise product quality so as to successfully promote the region to the upper end of the market range;
- Ensure that the region's destinations are effectively managed.

Sustainability, the first aim, is a key priority for the future development of tourism in the South West. SWT is encouraging travel and tourism organisations in the region to join its Green Tourism Business Scheme, integrating its Green Awareness Training into their own staff development programmes.

Issues to consider

1. There is increased concern among the travelling public about the carbon footprint left by increasing numbers of air journeys.

CONSIDER: How this concern may impact on the future development of tourism in the South West (both positively and negatively).

2. The South West has traditionally been seen as a largely leisure tourism (holidays) destination.

CONSIDER: The scope for marketing business tourism to the South West of England.

3. Cultural tourism market sectors that are important to the South West region include the arts, film and television, crafts, festivals and special events, heritage attractions and museums.

CONSIDER: Why South West Tourism should regard cultural tourism as particularly important to the future development of tourism in its region.

Discussion questions

(differentiated by level)

1. Many visitors to the South West are touring or self-packaging. They are often from different regions of the UK. Describe the range of tourist information opportunities provided and explain the usefulness of each to tourists visiting the South West of England (Level3/GCE AS).
2. Suggest how accommodation providers in the South West can develop their businesses sustainably (Level 3/GCE AS).
3. Virtually all communities in the South West experience some direct, indirect and induced impacts of tourism. Analyse the range of positive and negative impacts affecting a tourist region such as the South West (Level 3/GCE A2).
4. Propose and justify a range of stakeholder groups that should be represented on a Regional Tourist Board such as that of South West Tourism (Foundation Degree).

15

Thomson /TUI

– a mass-market tour operator

Introduction

Thomson Holidays is a mass-market tour operator. It is part of TUI Travel plc, which was formed in 2007 by the merger of TUI UK Ltd, which included Thomson, and another large-scale UK-based tour operator, First Choice Holidays.

Thomson packages a wide variety of holiday products to short and long-haul destinations and sells high volumes on the mainstream holidays market. So, it is referred to as a 'mass-market' tour operator, while Kuoni (see Case Study 3), for example, is primarily a long-haul tour operator and Lynchpin (see Case Study 4) is a small-scale, specialist tour operator.

History and development

In 1965, at the height of the boom in demand for package holidays to the sun, entrepreneur Lord Thomson bought three travel and tourism companies – the charter airline Britannia Airways and the tour operators Riviera Holidays and Universal Skytours. His companies continued to trade successfully, as demand for package holidays continued to rise. By the late 1960s, Thomson had introduced winter sun, cruise and lakes and mountains package holidays to the UK mass market.

It was not, however, until 1972 that the brand name Thomson Holidays was created. In that year, Lord Thomson combined his tour operating brands into one tour operating company – Thomson Holidays. He kept the name Britannia Airways for the charter airline that Thomson package holiday customers used. The package holidays market was continuing to grow rapidly and Thomson Holidays grew with it. By 1974, two more companies, Sunair and the high street travel agent Lunn Poly, had been brought into the Thomson fold. Thomson Holidays had now become the UK's largest vertically-integrated travel company, carrying out tour operator, transport principal and travel agent functions, as Figure 15.1 shows.

In 2007, TUI (Thomson's parent company) and the rival mass-market tour operator First Choice Holidays merged. This was the same year as the merger between Thomas Cook and MyTravel (see Case Study 1). The UK's 'big four' tour operators had suddenly, and very quickly, become just two.

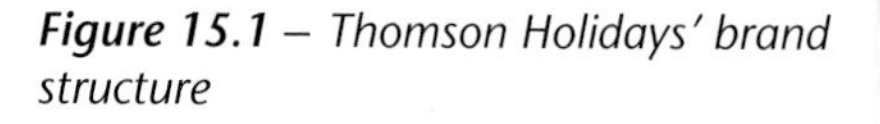
***Figure 15.1** – Thomson Holidays' brand structure*

Structure

TUI Travel, formed from the merger of TUI UK and First Choice, is part of the international company TUI AG. TUI AG is a large international corporation, which originated in Germany. It is now the largest tourism and services group in the world. Globally, TUI employs 80,000 people in 500 branded companies.

Thomson Holidays' head office is in Luton, Bedfordshire. Its UK retail distribution channels include:

- Thomson travel agencies – over 730 retail stores in the UK;
- Thomson's UK call centre operation;
- Thomson's website www.thomson.co.uk, where customers can research, book and pay for holidays online.

Through these channels, Thomson sells around 5 million holidays and flights a year.

As well as the main Thomson tour operating brand, Thomson's portfolio also includes several specialist and niche holiday brands, including Jetsave, Jersey Travel, Simply Travel, Headwater Holidays, the Magic Travel Group, Crystal Holidays, Thomson Ski and Snowboarding, and Thomson Lakes and Mountains.

Thomsonfly.com and Portland Direct, a direct sales tour operating business with its own website www.portlandholidays.co.uk, are sister companies of Thomson Holidays within the TUI group. Thomsonfly.com operates flights from 24 UK airports to over 80 destinations around the world. Based at London Luton Airport, the airline, which was formerly known as Britannia Airways, carried 5 million passengers in 2006 and is now the UK's third largest carrier.

***Figure 15.2** – Thomsonfly is part of the TUI group of companies*

Operations

Thomson Holidays publishes a wide range of holiday brochures to market its holiday packages under the Thomson brand name and others such as Headwater and Magic. Thomson Holidays is the market leader in the UK air-inclusive holiday market, a position it has held since 1974. The company operates over 700 travel agent shops in the UK, its own website www.thomson.co.uk for online bookings, a UK call centre, cruise ships and its own promotional digital television channel. The Thomsonfly.com airline, is a fellow member of the TUI group. Thomson aims to provide products and services to meet the needs of a wide range of customers, "whether it's a one-way flight to Malaga, two nights at a city centre hotel in Paris, a villa in Italy or a five star tailor-made trip to Australia." The website allows customers to self-package their holiday from component menus of flights, holidays, hotels, villas, apartments and attractions for destinations and lengths of stay that they choose.

The company has approximately one-third of the UK tour operations' market. Its management claim that Thomson generates more repeat business from satisfied, past customers than any other UK holiday company. Operational strategies that Thomson Holidays uses to build customer confidence include:

- A 'Moneyback Guarantee' – if Thomson are not able to resolve a travelling customer's issue or complaint within 24 hours, the customer can be flown home at the company's expense. Thomson will also refund the cost of the aborted holiday. There are some exceptions, for example from ski and snowboarding holidays;
- 'No Worries Guarantee' – Resort representatives are required to address customer complaints within a benchmark time of 1 hour. Similar exceptions apply as to the money back guarantee, for example on long-haul Thomson Worldwide holidays;
- '24-hour Holiday Line' – Thomson operates a 24-hour customer telephone helpline.

In addition, all hotel and apartment accommodation is examined on behalf of Thomson by a UK-qualified safety inspector.

Thomson Holidays operate co-operatively with other TUI Group members. For example, they make use of sister company Thomsonfly's 47 aircraft, which carry over 8 million passengers per year from the UK to over 80 destinations in 37 countries. Thomson resort representatives also look after Portland Direct customers in-resort on behalf of that TUI Group sister company. Thomson resort representatives ensure Portland's customers are picked up at the airport, as they do for Thomson Holidays' own customers, and invite them to attend the welcome meeting. Portland Direct customers are also able to use the Thomson 24-hour telephone helpline.

Staffing

Altogether, the TUI Group employs some 17,500 people in the UK, Ireland and Scandinavia. Of these, 3,000 work for Thomson Holidays. Although the Thomson's head office is in Luton, most staff work abroad, for example as resort representatives. Thomsonfly has been awarded the Investors in People (IIP) award in recognition of the quality of its training and staff development programme. By 2007, the award had been renewed twice and at that time Thomsonfly remained the only major UK airline to hold the IIP award.

As a whole, TUI Group had 53,930 employees in 2006, 14.3% less than in 2005. The tourism division continued to employ the largest proportion of staff (82.3%), up 2.1% since 2005. However, the total number of employees in TUI's tourism businesses was 44,409 in 2006, which was 12.1% down on 2005. The number of employees in TUI's destinations was, however, 7.1% up at 13,783. TUI personnel data are shown in Figure 15.3.

Tourism Division	**44,409**
Central Europe	9,411
Northern Europe	14,711
Western Europe	6,504
Destinations	13,783
Other tourism	-
Shipping	**8,571**
Central Operations	**950**
TOTAL	**53,930**

***Figure 15.3** – TUI group personnel data 2006*

Funding and finance

The First Choice and TUI/Thomson merger of 2007 was made possible by a major refinancing package. A £1.2 billion credit facility was put in place to enable TUI to borrow funds to facilitate the joining together of the two major mass-market tour operating concerns.

Financial results for the trading quarter immediately before the September merger showed a 9.4% drop in turnover to 1.12 billion Euros for TUI's Northern Europe division, which includes the UK and Ireland. Earnings were down 79 million Euros year-on-year from a profit of 43 million Euros to a loss of 36 million Euros. This was despite a 1.7% rise in air passenger numbers to 1.88 million, mainly driven by Thomsonfly's seat-only sales.

Marketing

Thomson Holidays makes extensive use of its customer base for market research purposes. Every Thomson customer is asked to complete a feedback questionnaire on their return flight home. Responses are analysed by independent market researchers. Hotel and other accommodation providers which are scored sufficiently highly by customers receive a Thomson Holidays Gold Medal award. This is then shown in the following year's brochure, promoting the accommodation Thomson customers liked and conveying a marketing message of trustworthiness to brochure browsers. In addition, customer opinion scores are published on brochure accommodation pages.

The successful placement of Thomson Holidays products in the market place is achieved through:

- Published brochures, which are stocked by Thomson's own travel agent shops and by those of other travel agency organisations;
- Increasingly, the Thomson website www.thomson.co.uk;
- Thomson's own digital television channel;
- Advertising and promotional campaigns.

The TUI logo has been increasingly deployed to build the image of a single company in the minds of its potential customers. The re-branding

Figure 15.4 – A Thomson travel agency

of Lunn Poly travel agent shops as Thomson (Figure 15.4) has also been an important part of this process.

At what is currently a time of increased awareness of sustainable development and environmental conservation issues, Thomson Holidays uses the sustainable tourism section of its website to promote the organisation's 'green credentials'. This is done by showing ways that Thomson operates to protect destinations' environments, communities and wildlife, and to help Thomson customers travel responsibly.

Future

Following the 2007 merger between Thomson/TUI and First Choice, Thomson Holidays expects to grow still larger. Cost efficiencies that have been achieved by combining the two tour operating businesses are expected to enable TUI/Thomson to acquire more businesses and expand as an integrated travel and tourism organisation.

Revenues in the company's online destination services business increased by 42% in 2006-7 and this aspect of the business is likely to show continued growth as independent tour operators, travel agents and travellers take further advantage of dynamic and self-packaging opportunities. The www.thomson.co.uk website will be an important tool as the conventional package holiday business continues to shrink.

Specialist markets are likely to continue expanding too. Revenues from activity holidays have recently risen by 3% per annum, while strong demand for specialist holidays has seen turnover rising by 15% per year and the volume of trade in niche markets swell by 13%. As the market in conventional general interest package holidays dwindles, because customers increasingly make their own arrangements, it is in the specialist and activity sectors that future consumers are likely to still value the role of tour operators.

Environmental awareness and concerns about the negative impacts of tourism are likely to become even more embedded in the public consciousness in the near-future. Thomson is likely to feel continued commercial pressure to be seen to operate sustainable business practices in destinations, to conserve the environment and to minimise the consumption of energy and other resources. In 2007, Thomsonfly confirmed that it would be seeking to operate the latest, most fuel-efficient planes into the future, beginning with new Boeing 787 Dreamliner aircraft.

Issues to consider

1. Since the Thomson/TUI and First Choice merger of 2007, TUI Travel UK, including Thomson Holidays, plans to operate both Thomson and First Choice brands on the high street and overseas.

CONSIDER: The advantages and disadvantages to the Thomson Holidays' business of this policy decision.

2. Cost efficiencies have come from the 2007 merger.

CONSIDER: (a) the likely sources of such savings; (b) how they may affect future job opportunities in the UK tour operating sector.

3. The internet and e-commerce are likely to continue to grow in their importance to Thomson Holidays. In TUI Group's Mainstream Holidays Sector, which includes Thomson, over 25% of bookings are now made online.

CONSIDER: How Thomson can adapt to keep up with the continued development of the internet.

4. "Beautiful destinations are at the heart of travel, so it is vital to sustain these environments for future generations and the people who live there."

CONSIDER: The role of major travel companies such as Thomson/TUI in the sustainable management of holiday destinations.

Discussion questions

(differentiated by level)

1. Suggest reasons for recent changes in the number of staff employed by Thomson (Level3/GCE AS).

2. Assess the impact of internet growth on the future of the package holiday (Level3/GCE A2).

3. Small travel companies (like Lynchpin in Case Study 4) thrive in specialist and niche markets. Major companies like Thomson/TUI continue to grow by acquisition and integration. Discuss the extent and implications of such apparent polarisation in the travel and tourism industry (Foundation Degree).

Index